The Mother's Topical Bible

DIVINE TRUTH AND WISDOM FOR
NAVIGATING THE JOURNEY OF
MOTHERHOOD

RACINE, WI

The Mother's Topical Bible
ISBN: 979-8-88898-063-7 - *Paperback*
ISBN: 979-8-88898-064-4 - *Hardcover*
ISBN: 979-8-88898-065-1 - *Ebook*
Copyright © 2023 by Honor Books, Racine, WI

Cover Design by Faille Schmitz. Compiled by Mike Murdock.
All Scripture references are from the King James Version of the Bible

Contents

WHEN YOUR CHILD . . .

WHEN YOUR HUSBAND . . .

YOUR WORK

YOUR DAILY SCHEDULE

YOUR FINANCES

YOUR ROLE IN THE CHURCH

YOUR PERSONAL NEEDS

The Virtuous Woman

PROVERBS 31:10-31

[10]WHO CAN FIND A VIRTUOUS WOMAN? FOR HER PRICE IS FAR ABOVE RUBIES.

[11]The heart of her husband doth safely trust in her, so that he shall have no need of spoil.

[12]She will do him good and not evil all the days of her life.

[13]She seeketh wool, and flax, and worketh willingly with her hands.

[14]She is like the merchants' ships; she bringeth her food from afar.

[15]She riseth also while it is yet night, and giveth meat to her household, and a portion to her maidens.

[16]She considereth a field, and buyeth it: with the fruit of her hands she planteth a vineyard.

[17]She girdeth her loins with strength, and strengtheneth her arms.

[18]She perceiveth that her merchandise is good: her candle goeth not out by night.

[19]She layeth her hands to the spindle, and her hands hold the distaff.

[20]She stretcheth out her hand to the poor; yea, she reacheth forth her hands to the needy.

[21]She is not afraid of the snow for her household: for all her household are clothed with scarlet.

[22]She maketh herself coverings of tapestry; her clothing is silk and purple.

[23]Her husband is known in the gates, when he sitteth among the elders of the land.

[24]She maketh fine linen, and selleth it; and delivereth girdles unto the merchant.

[25]Strength and honour are her clothing; and she shall rejoice in time to come.

[26]She openeth her mouth with wisdom; and in her tongue is the law of kindness.

[27]She looketh well to the ways of her household, and eateth not the bread of idleness.

[28]Her children arise up, and call her blessed; her husband also, and he praiseth her.

[29]Many daughters have done virtuously, but thou excellest them all.

[30]Favour is deceitful, and beauty is vain: but a woman that feareth the Lord, she shall be praised.

[31]Give her of the fruit of her hands; and let her own works praise her in the gates.

The Salvation Experience

THREE BASIC REASONS TO
BELIEVE THE BIBLE IS THE
INFALLIBLE AND PURE
WORD OF GOD

1. *No human would have written a standard this high.* Think of the best person you know. You must admit he would have left certain scriptures out had he written the Bible. So the Bible projects an inhuman standard and way of life. It has to be God because no man you know would have ever written a standard that high.

2. *There is an aura, a climate, a charisma, a presence the Bible generates which no other book in the world creates.* Lay an encyclopedia on your table at the restaurant, nobody will look at you twice. But when you lay your Bible on the table, they will stare at you, watch you chew your food, and even read your license plate when you get in your car! Why? The Bible creates the presence of God and forces a reaction in the hearts of men.

3. *The nature of man is changed when he reads the Bible.* Men change. Peace enters into their spirits. Joy wells up within their lives. Men like what they become when they read this book. Men accept Christ, because this Bible says Jesus Christ is the Son of God and that all have sinned and the wages of sin will bring death; and the only forgiveness that they can find is through Jesus, the Son of God.

Three Basic Reasons for Accepting Christ

THE SALVATION EXPERIENCE

1. *You needed forgiveness.* At some point in your life, you will want to be clean. You will hate guilt; you will crave purity. You have a built-in desire toward God, and you will have to address that appetite at some point in your life.

2. *You need a friend.* You may be sitting there saying, "But, don't I have friends?" Yes, but you have never had a friend like Jesus. Nobody can handle the information about your life as well as He can. He is the most consistent relationship you will ever know. Human friends vacillate in their reaction, depending on your mood or theirs. Jesus Christ never changes his opinion of you. Nobody can tell Him anything which will change His mind about you. You cannot enjoy His world without His companionship.

3. *You needed a future.* All men have a built-in need for immortality, a craving for an eternity. God placed it within us. D.L. Moody once made a statement, "One of these days you are going to hear that I'm dead and gone. When you do, don't believe a word of it. I'll be more alive then, than at any other time in my life." Each of us wonders about eternity. What is death like? What happens when I die? Is there a hell? a heaven? a God? a devil? What happens? Every man wants to be around tomorrow. The only guarantee you will have of a future is to have the Eternal One on the inside of you. *He is Jesus Christ, the Son of God!*

The Gospel means Good News, you can change; your sins can be forgiven; your guilt can be dissolved; God loves you! He wants to be the difference in your life. All have sinned and come short of the glory of God." Romans 3:23. "The wages of sin is death." Romans 6:23. You might say, what does that mean? It means that all unconfessed sin will be judged and penalized, but that is not the end of the story. The second part of verse 23 says "but the gift of God is eternal life through Jesus Christ our Lord." What does that mean? It means that between the wrath and judgment of God upon your sin, Jesus Christ the Son of God stepped in and absorbed your judgment and your penalty for you. God says if you recognize and respect Him and His worth as the Son of God, judgment will be withheld, and you will receive a pardon, forgiveness of all your mistakes.

What do you have to do? "If you believe in your heart that Jesus is the Son of God and that God raised him from the dead on the third day, and confess that with your mouth, then you will be saved." Romans 10:9-10. What does the word "saved" mean? Removed from danger. It simply means if you respect and recognize the worth of Jesus Christ, God will take you out of the danger zone and receive you as a child of the Most High God. What is His gift that you are to receive? His Son. "For God so loved the world that he gave his only begotten Son, that whosoever believeth in Him should not perish but have everlasting life." John 3:16. How do you accept His Son? Accept His mercy. How do you reject your sins? Confess them and turn away from them. "If I confess my sins he is faithful and just to forgive me my sins and to cleanse me from all unrighteousness." 1 John 1:9. That is the Gospel.

Your Relationship with God

YOUR PRAYER LIFE

If my people, which are called by my name, shall humble themselves, and pray, and seek my face, and turn from their wicked ways; then will I hear from heaven, and will forgive their sin, and will heal their land.
2 CHRONICLES 7:14

When thou saidst, Seek ye my face; my heart said unto thee, Thy face, Lord, will I seek.
PSALM 27:8

As for me, I will call upon God; and the Lord shall save me. Evening, and morning, and at noon, will I pray, and cry aloud: and he shall hear my voice.
PSALM 55:16-17

Glory ye in his holy name: let the heart of them rejoice that seek the Lord. Seek the Lord, and his strength: seek his face evermore.
PSALM 105:3-4

The Lord is nigh unto all them that call upon him, to all that call upon him in truth.
PSALM 145:18

But thou, when thou prayest, enter into thy closet, and when thou hast shut thy door, pray to thy Father which is in secret; and thy Father which seeth in secret shall reward thee openly.
MATTHEW 6:6

Likewise the Spirit also helpeth our infirmities: for we
know not what we should pray for as we ought: but the
Spirit itself maketh intercession for us with groanings
which cannot be uttered.
ROMANS 8:26

Praying always with all prayer and supplication in the
Spirit, and watching thereunto with all perseverance and
supplication for all saints.
EPHESIANS 6:18

Be careful for nothing; but in every thing by prayer and
supplication with thanksgiving let your requests be made
known unto God.
PHILIPPIANS 4:6

Continue in prayer, and watch in the same with thanksgiving.
COLOSSIANS 4:2

Pray without ceasing.
1 THESSALONIANS 5:17

I will therefore that men pray every where, lifting up holy
hands, without wrath and doubting.
1 TIMOTHY 2:8

Let us therefore come boldly unto the throne of grace,
that we may obtain mercy, and find grace to help in time
of need.
HEBREWS 4:16

And he spake a parable unto them to this end, that men ought always to pray, and not to faint.

LUKE 18:1

Seek ye the Lord while he may be found, call ye upon him while he is near.
ISAIAH 55:6

For the eyes of the Lord are over the righteous, and his ears are open unto their prayers: but the face of the Lord is against them that do evil.
1 PETER 3:12

But ye, beloved, building up yourselves on your most holy faith, praying in the Holy Ghost.
JUDE 1:20

Your Study of God's Word

YOUR RELATIONSHIP WITH GOD

And Moses came and told the people all the words of the Lord, and all the judgments: and all the people answered with one voice, and said, All the words which the Lord hath said will we do.
EXODUS 24:3

Ye shall not add unto the word which I command you, neither shall ye diminish ought from it, that ye may keep the commandments of the Lord your God which I command you.
DEUTERONOMY 4:2

And these words, which I command thee this day, shall be in thine heart.
DEUTERONOMY 6:6

And he humbled thee, and suffered thee to hunger, and fed thee with manna, which thou knewest not, neither did thy fathers know; that he might make thee know that man doth not live by bread only, but by every word that proceedeth out of the mouth of the Lord doth man live.
DEUTERONOMY 8:3

But the word is very nigh unto thee, in thy mouth, and
in thy heart, that thou mayest do it.
DEUTERONOMY 30:14

This book of the law shall not depart out of thy mouth;
but thou shalt meditate therein day and night, that thou
mayest observe to do according to all that is written
therein: for then thou shalt make thy way prosperous, and
then thou shalt have good success.
JOSHUA 1:8

Be ye mindful always of his covenant; the word which he
commanded to a thousand generations.
1 CHRONICLES 16:15

Receive, I pray thee, the law from his mouth, and lay up
his words in thine heart.
JOB 22:22

Neither have I gone back from the commandment of his
lips; I have esteemed the words of his mouth more than
my necessary food.
JOB 23:12

But his delight is in the law of the Lord; and in his law
doth he meditate day and night.
PSALM 1:2

The law of the Lord is perfect, converting the soul: the
testimony of the Lord is sure, making wise the simple.
PSALM 19:7

I will instruct thee and teach thee in the way which thou
shalt go: I will guide thee with mine eye.
PSALM 32:8

The law of his God is in his heart; none of his steps shall
slide.
PSALM 37:31

When thou goest, it shall lead thee; when thou sleepest,
it shall keep thee; and when thou awakest, it shall talk
with thee. For the commandment is a lamp; and the law
is light; and reproofs of instruction are the way of life.
PROVERBS 6:22-23

Therefore whosoever heareth these sayings of mine, and
doeth them, I will liken him unto a wise man, which built
his house upon a rock.
MATTHEW 7:24

Jesus answered and said unto them, Ye do err, not knowing
the scriptures, nor the power of God.
MATTHEW 22:29

Then said Jesus to those Jews which believed on him, If
ye continue in my word, then are ye my disciples indeed;
And ye shall know the truth, and the truth shall make you
free.
JOHN 8:31-32

Thy word have I hid in mine heart, that I might not sin against thee. Thy word is a lamp unto my feet, and a light unto my path.

PSALM 119:11,105

Heaven and earth shall pass away: but my words shall not pass away.
MARK 13:31

So then faith cometh by hearing, and hearing by the word of God.
ROMANS 10:17

All scripture is given by inspiration of God, and is profitable for doctrine, for reproof, for correction, for instruction in righteousness: That the man of God may be perfect, throughly furnished unto all good works.
2 TIMOTHY 3:16-17

Your Attitude Toward Praise and Worship

YOUR RELATIONSHIP WITH GOD

I will call on the Lord, who is worthy to be praised: so shall I be saved from mine enemies.
2 SAMUEL 22:4

Give unto the Lord the glory due unto his name: bring an offering, and come before him: worship the Lord in the beauty of holiness.
1 CHRONICLES 16:29

It came even to pass, as the trumpeters and singers were as one, to make one sound to be heard in praising and thanking the Lord; and when they lifted up their voice with the trumpets and cymbals and instruments of music, and praised the Lord, saying, For he is good; for his mercy endureth for ever: that then the house was filled with a cloud, even the house of the Lord.
2 CHRONICLES 5:13

I will give thee thanks in the great congregation: I will praise thee among much people.
PSALM 35:18

Blessed are they that dwell in thy house: they will be still
praising thee.
PSALM 84:4

It is a good thing to give thanks unto the Lord, and to
sing praises unto thy name, O most High.
PSALM 92:1

O come, let us worship and bow down: let us kneel before
the Lord our maker.
PSALM 95:6

Make a joyful noise unto the Lord, all ye lands.
Serve the Lord with gladness: come before his presence
with singing. Know ye that the Lord he is God: it is he
that hath made us, and not we ourselves; we are his people,
and the sheep of his pasture. Enter into his gates with
thanksgiving, and into his courts with praise: be thankful
unto him, and bless his name.
PSALM 100:1-4

Oh that men would praise the Lord for his goodness, and
for his wonderful works to the children of men!
Let them exalt him also in the congregation of the people,
and praise him in the assembly of the elders.
PSALM 107:8,32

I will worship toward thy holy temple, and praise thy name for thy lovingkindness and for thy truth: for thou hast magnified thy word above all thy name.
PSALM 138:2

But the hour cometh, and now is, when the true worshippers shall worship the Father in spirit and in truth: for the Father seeketh such to worship him.
God is a Spirit: and they that worship him must worship him in spirit and in truth.
JOHN 4:23-24

What is it then? I will pray with the spirit, and I will pray with the understanding also: I will sing with the spirit, and I will sing with the understanding also.
1 CORINTHIANS 14:15

I will therefore that men pray every where, lifting up holy hands, without wrath and doubting.
1 TIMOTHY 2:8

Ye also, as lively stones, are built up a spiritual house, an holy priesthood, to offer up spiritual sacrifices, acceptable to God by Jesus Christ.
1 PETER 2:5

... they rest not day and night, saying, "Holy, holy, holy, Lord God Almighty, which was, and is, and is to come."

REVELATION 4:8

Praise ye the Lord. Praise God in his sanctuary: praise him in the firmament of his power.
Praise him for his mighty acts: praise him according to his excellent greatness.
Praise him with the sound of the trumpet: praise him with the psaltery and harp.
Praise him with the timbrel and dance: praise him with stringed instruments and organs.
Praise him upon the loud cymbals: praise him upon the high sounding cymbals. Let every thing that hath breath praise the Lord. Praise ye the Lord.

PSALM 150:1-3,5,6

Your Hourly Obedience to God

YOUR RELATIONSHIP WITH GOD

Now therefore, if ye will obey my voice indeed, and keep
my covenant, then ye shall be a peculiar treasure unto me
above all people: for all the earth is mine.
EXODUS 19:5

And if thou wilt walk in my ways, to keep my statutes
and my commandments, as thy father David did walk,
then I will lengthen thy days.
1 KINGS 3:14

Blessed is the man that walketh not in the counsel of the
ungodly, nor standeth in the way of sinners, nor sitteth
in the seat of the scornful. But his delight is in the law
of the Lord; and in his law doth he meditate day and night.
PSALM 1:1-2

All the paths of the Lord are mercy and truth unto such
as keep his covenant and his testimonies.
PSALM 25:10

The fear of the Lord is the beginning of wisdom: a good
understanding have all they that do his commandments:
his praise endureth for ever.
PSALM 111:10

If ye be willing and obedient, ye shall eat the good of the land.
ISAIAH 1:19

Whosoever therefore shall break one of these least commandments, and shall teach men so, he shall be called the least in the kingdom of heaven: but whosoever shall do and teach them, the same shall be called great in the kingdom of heaven.
MATTHEW 5:19

For whosoever shall do the will of my Father which is in heaven, the same is my brother, and sister, and mother.
MATTHEW 12:50

If ye love me, keep my commandments.
Jesus answered and said unto him, If a man love me, he will keep my words: and my Father will love him, and we will come unto him, and make our abode with him.
JOHN 14:15,23

If ye keep my commandments, ye shall abide in my love; even as I have kept my Father's commandments, and abide in his love.
Ye are my friends, if ye do whatsoever I command you.
JOHN 15:10,14

And whatsoever we ask, we receive of him, because we keep his commandments, and do those things that are pleasing in his sight.
1 JOHN 3:22

When You Want to Be...

A PATIENT MOTHER

Rest in the Lord, and wait patiently for him: fret not thyself because of him who prospereth in his way, because of the man who bringeth wicked devices to pass.
PSALM 37:7

I waited patiently for the Lord; and he inclined unto me, and heard my cry.
PSALM 40:1

For thou art my hope, O Lord God: thou art my trust from my youth.
PSALM 71:5

I can do all things through Christ which strengtheneth me.
PHILIPPIANS 4:13

Better is the end of a thing than the beginning thereof: and the patient in spirit is better than the proud in spirit. Be not hasty in thy spirit to be angry: for anger resteth in the bosom of fools.
ECCLESIASTES 7:8-9

But they that wait upon the Lord shall renew their strength; they shall mount up with wings as eagles; they shall run, and not be weary; and they shall walk, and not faint.
ISAIAH 40:31

Blessed is the man that trusteth in the Lord, and whose hope the Lord is.
JEREMIAH 17:7

In your patience possess ye your souls.
LUKE 21:19

And not only so, but we glory in tribulations also: knowing
that tribulation worketh patience;
And patience, experience; and experience, hope:
And hope maketh not ashamed; because the love of God
is shed abroad in our hearts by the Holy Ghost which is
given unto us.
ROMANS 5:3-5

But if we hope for that we see not, then do we with patience
wait for it.
ROMANS 8:25

For whatsoever things were written aforetime were written
for our learning, that we through patience and comfort
of the scriptures might have hope. Now the God of
patience and consolation grant you to be likeminded one
toward another according to Christ Jesus . . . Now the
God of hope fill you with all joy and peace in believing,
that ye may abound in hope, through the power of the
Holy Ghost.
ROMANS 15:4-5,13

But the fruit of the Spirit is love, joy, peace, long-suffering,
gentleness, goodness, faith.
GALATIANS 5:22

Knowing this, that the trying of your faith worketh
patience. But let patience have her perfect work, that ye
may be perfect and entire, wanting nothing.
JAMES 1:3-4

And beside this, giving all diligence, add to your faith
virtue; and to virtue knowledge; And to knowledge temperance; and to temperance patience; and to patience
godliness.
2 PETER 1:5-6

That ye be not slothful, but followers of them who through faith and patience inherit the promises.

HEBREWS 6:12

Cast not away therefore your confidence, which hath great recompence of reward. For ye have need of patience, that, after ye have done the will of God, ye might receive the promise. For yet a little while, and he that shall come will come, and will not tarry.
HEBREWS 10:35-37

Be patient therefore, brethren, unto the coming of the Lord. Behold, the husbandman waiteth for the precious fruit of the earth, and hath long patience for it, until he receive the early and latter rain. Be ye also patient; stablish your hearts: for the coming of the Lord draweth nigh.
JAMES 5:7-8

A Loving Mother

Owe no man any thing, but to love one another: for he
that loveth another hath fulfilled the law.
Love worketh no ill to his neighbour: therefore love is the
fulfilling of the law.
ROMANS 13:8,10

Though I speak with the tongues of men and of angels,
and have not charity, I am become as sounding brass, or
a tinkling cymbal. And though I have the gift of prophecy,
and understand all mysteries, and all knowledge; and
though I have all faith, so that I could remove mountains,
and have not charity, I am nothing.
And though I bestow all my goods to feed the poor, and
though I give my body to be burned, and have not charity,
it profiteth me nothing.
Charity suffereth long, and is kind; charity envieth not;
charity vaunteth not itself, is not puffed up, Doth not
behave itself unseemly, seeketh not her own, is not easily
provoked, thinketh no evil;
Rejoiceth not in iniquity, but rejoiceth in the truth;
Beareth all things, believeth all things, hopeth all things,
endureth all things.
Charity never faileth.
1 CORINTHIANS 13:1-8A

Hatred stirreth up strifes: but love covereth all sins.
PROVERBS 10:12

Many waters cannot quench love, neither can the floods drown it: if a man would give all the substance of his house for love, it would utterly be contemned.
SONG OF SOLOMON 8:7

A new commandment I give unto you, That ye love one another; as I have loved you, that ye also love one another. By this shall all men know that ye are my disciples, if ye have love one to another.
JOHN 13:34-35

As the Father hath loved me, so have I loved you: continue ye in my love.
If ye keep my commandments, ye shall abide in my love; even as I have kept my Father's commandments, and abide in his love.
This is my commandment, That ye love one another, as I have loved you.
Greater love hath no man than this, that a man lay down his life for his friends.
Ye are my friends, if ye do whatsoever I command you. Henceforth I call you not servants; for the servant knoweth not what his lord doeth: but I have called you friends; for all things that I have heard of my Father I have made known unto you.
Ye have not chosen me, but I have chosen you, and ordained you, that ye should go and bring forth fruit, and that your fruit should remain: that whatsoever ye shall ask of the Father in my name, he may give it you.
These things I command you, that ye love one another.
JOHN 15:9-10,12-17

And now abideth faith, hope, charity, these three; but the greatest of these is charity.
1 CORINTHIANS 13:13

And walk in love, as Christ also hath loved us, and hath given himself for us an offering and a sacrifice to God for a sweet-smelling savour.
EPHESIANS 5:2

And the Lord make you to increase and abound in love one toward another, and toward all men, even as we do toward you.
1 THESSALONIANS 3:12

For God is not unrighteous to forget your work and labour of love, which ye have shewed toward his name, in that ye have ministered to the saints, and do minister.
HEBREWS 6:10

And let us consider one another to provoke unto love and to good works.
HEBREWS 10:24

If ye fulfill the royal law according to the scripture, Thou shalt love thy neighbour as thyself, ye do well.
JAMES 2:8

We know that we have passed from death unto life, because we love the brethren. He that loveth not his brother abideth in death.
1 JOHN 3:14

For this is the message that ye heard from the beginning, that we should love one another.

1 JOHN 3:11

My little children, let us not love in word, neither in tongue; but in deed and in truth.
1 JOHN 3:18

Beloved, let us love one another: for love is of God; and every one that loveth is born of God, and knoweth God. He that loveth not knoweth not God; for God is love.
1 JOHN 4:7-8

And above all things have fervent charity among yourselves: for charity shall cover the multitude of sins.
1 PETER 4:8

A Giving Mother

Bring ye all the tithes into the storehouse, that there may
be meat in mine house, and prove me now herewith, saith
the Lord of hosts, if I will not open you the windows of
heaven, and pour you out a blessing, that there shall not
be room enough to receive it.
And I will rebuke the devourer for your sakes, and he shall
not destroy the fruits of your ground; neither shall your
vine cast her fruit before the time in the field, saith the
Lord of hosts.
And all nations shall call you blessed: for ye shall be a
delightsome land, saith the Lord of hosts.
MALACHI 3:10-12

Be ye strong therefore, and let not your hands be weak:
for your work shall be rewarded.
2 CHRONICLES 15:7

A good man sheweth favour, and lendeth: he will guide
his affairs with discretion.
PSALM 112:5

Honour the Lord with thy substance, and with the firstfruits
of all thine increase:
So shall thy barns be filled with plenty, and thy presses
shall burst out with new wine.
PROVERBS 3:9-10

He that hath pity upon the poor lendeth unto the Lord;
and that which he hath given will he pay him again.
PROVERBS 19:17

He that hath a bountiful eye shall be blessed; for he giveth
of his bread to the poor.
PROVERBS 22:9

He that giveth unto the poor shall not lack: but he that
hideth his eyes shall have many a curse.
PROVERBS 28:27

And every one that hath forsaken houses, or brethren, or
sisters, or father, or mother, or wife, or children, or lands,
for my name's sake, shall receive an hundredfold, and shall
inherit everlasting life.
MATTHEW 19:29

Give, and it shall be given unto you; good measure, pressed
down, and shaken together, and running over, shall men
give into your bosom. For with the same measure that ye
mete withal it shall be measured to you again.
LUKE 6:38

Upon the first day of the week let every one of you lay
by him in store, as God hath prospered him, that there be
no gatherings when I come.
1 CORINTHIANS 16:2

But this I say, He which soweth sparingly shall reap also
sparingly; and he which soweth bountifully shall reap also
bountifully.
Every man according as he purposeth in his heart, so let
him give; not grudgingly, or of necessity: for God loveth
a cheerful giver.
And God is able to make all grace abound toward you;
that ye, always having all sufficiency in all things, may
abound to every good work:
2 CORINTHIANS 9:6-8

Charge them that are rich in this world, that they be not
highminded, nor trust in uncertain riches, but in the living
God, who giveth us richly all things to enjoy;
That they do good, that they be rich in good works, ready
to distribute, willing to communicate;
Laying up in store for themselves a good foundation
against the time to come, that they may lay hold on eternal
life.
1 TIMOTHY 6:17-19

Beloved, I wish above all things that thou mayest prosper
and be in health, even as thy soul prospereth.
3 JOHN 2

Heal the sick, cleanse the lepers, raise the dead, cast out devils: freely ye have received, freely give.

MATTHEW 10:8

Cast thy bread upon the waters: for thou shalt find it after many days.
ECCLESIASTES 11:1

But whoso hath this world's good, and seeth his brother have need, and shutteth up his bowels of compassion from him, how dwelleth the love of God in him?
My little children, let us not love in word, neither in tongue; but in deed and in truth.
1 JOHN 3:17-18

A Resourceful Mother

But there is a spirit in man: and the inspiration of the
Almighty giveth them understanding.
JOB 32:8

Then he openeth the ears of men, and sealeth their
instruction.
JOB 33:16

I will bless the Lord, who hath given me counsel: my reins
also instruct me in the night seasons.
PSALM 16:7

I will instruct thee and teach thee in the way which thou
shalt go: I will guide thee with mine eye.
PSALM 32:8

Behold, thou desirest truth in the inward parts: and in
the hidden part thou shalt make me to know wisdom.
PSALM 51:6

The Lord will perfect that which concerneth me: thy
mercy, O Lord, endureth for ever: forsake not the works
of thine own hands.
PSALM 138:8

Wisdom is the principal thing; therefore get wisdom: and
with all thy getting get understanding.
Exalt her, and she shall promote thee: she shall bring thee
to honour, when thou dost embrace her.
PROVERBS 4:7-8

I love them that love me; and those that seek me early
shall find me. Riches and honour are with me; yea, durable
riches and righteousness.
That I may cause those that love me to inherit substance;
and I will fill their treasures.
PROVERBS 8:17-18,21

The thoughts of the righteous are right: but the counsels
of the wicked are deceit.
PROVERBS 12:5

He that walketh with wise men shall be wise: but a
companion of fools shall be destroyed.
PROVERBS 13:20

A wise man will hear, and will increase learning; and a man of understanding shall attain unto wise counsels.
PROVERBS 1:5

So shall the knowledge of wisdom be unto thy soul: when thou hast found it, then there shall be a reward, and thy expectation shall not be cut off.
PROVERBS 24:14

Behold, the former things are come to pass, and new things do I declare: before they spring forth I tell you of them.
ISAIAH 42:9

Ask, and it shall be given you; seek, and ye shall find; knock, and it shall be opened unto you.
MATTHEW 7:7

For which of you, intending to build a tower, sitteth not down first, and counteth the cost, whether he have sufficient to finish it?
LUKE 14:28

If any of you lack wisdom, let him ask of God, that giveth to all men liberally, and upbraideth not; and it shall be given him.
JAMES 1:5

The fear of the Lord is the beginning of knowledge: but fools despise wisdom and instruction.

PROVERBS 1:7

A Godly Example as a Mother

And he did that which was right in the sight of the Lord,
according to all that David his father had done.
2 CHRONICLES 29:2

He that walketh with wise men shall be wise: but a
companion of fools shall be destroyed.
PROVERBS 13:20

And whosoever shall give to drink unto one of these little
ones a cup of cold water only in the name of a disciple,
verily I say unto you, he shall in no wise lose his reward.
MATTHEW 10:42

Even as the Son of man came not to be ministered unto,
but to minister, and to give his life a ransom for many.
MATTHEW 20:28

But so shall it not be among you: but whosoever will be great among you, shall be your minister: And whosoever of you will be the chiefest, shall be servant of all.
MARK 10:43-44

And he said, He that shewed mercy on him. Then said Jesus unto him, Go, and do thou likewise.
LUKE 10:37

For I have given you an example, that ye should do as I have done to you. Verily, verily, I say unto you, The servant is not greater than his lord; neither he that is sent greater than he that sent him.
A new commandment I give unto you, That ye love one another; as I have loved you, that ye also love one another.
JOHN 13:15-16,34

Now the God of patience and consolation grant you to be likeminded one toward another according to Christ Jesus: That ye may with one mind and one mouth glorify God, even the Father of our Lord Jesus Christ.
Wherefore receive ye one another, as Christ also received us to the glory of God.
ROMANS 15:5-7

Moreover it is required in stewards, that a man be found faithful.
1 CORINTHIANS 4:2

Bear ye one another's burdens, and so fulfill the law of Christ. As we have therefore opportunity, let us do good unto all men, especially unto them who are of the household of faith.
GALATIANS 6:2,10

Be ye therefore followers of God, as dear children; And walk in love, as Christ also hath loved us, and hath given himself for us an offering and a sacrifice to God for a sweet-smelling savour.
EPHESIANS 5:1-2

Servants, be obedient to them that are your masters according to the flesh, with fear and trembling, in singleness of your heart, as unto Christ; With good will doing service, as to the Lord, and not to men . . .
EPHESIANS 6:5-7

Let this mind be in you, which was also in Christ Jesus: Who, being in the form of God, thought it not robbery to be equal with God: But made himself of no reputation, and took upon him the form of a servant, and was made in the likeness of men: And being found in fashion as a man, he humbled himself, and became obedient unto death, even the death of the cross.
PHILIPPIANS 2:5-8

Hereby perceive we the love of God, because he laid down his life for us: and we ought to lay down our lives for the brethren.

1 JOHN 3:16

Forbearing one another, and forgiving one another, if any man have a quarrel against any: even as Christ forgave you, so also do ye.
Servants, obey in all things your masters according to the flesh; not with eye-service, as men-pleasers; but in singleness of heart, fearing God.
COLOSSIANS 3:13,22

For even hereunto were ye called: because Christ also suffered for us, leaving us an example, that ye should follow his steps.
1 PETER 2:21

For all that is in the world, the lust of the flesh, and the lust of the eyes, and the pride of life, is not of the Father, but is of the world.
1 JOHN 2:16

A Diligent Mother

Be ye strong therefore, and let not your hands be weak:
for your work shall be rewarded.
2 CHRONICLES 15:7

... and who knoweth whether thou art come to the kingdom for such a time as this?
ESTHER 4:14B

He that gathereth in summer is a wise son: but he that
sleepeth in harvest is a son that causeth shame.
PROVERBS 10:5

The hand of the diligent shall bear rule: but the slothful
shall be under tribute.
PROVERBS 12:24

The soul of the sluggard desireth, and hath nothing: but the soul of the diligent shall be made fat.

PROVERBS 13:4

The thoughts of the diligent tend only to plenteousness; but of every one that is hasty only to want.

PROVERBS 21:5

Seest thou a man diligent in his business? he shall stand before kings; he shall not stand before mean men.

PROVERBS 22:29

The Lord God is my strength, and he will make my feet like hinds' feet, and he will make me to walk upon mine high places.

HABAKKUK 3:19

Say not ye, There are yet four months, and then cometh harvest? behold, I say unto you, Lift up your eyes, and look on the fields; for they are white already to harvest.

JOHN 4:35

I must work the works of him that sent me, while it is
day: the night cometh, when no man can work.
JOHN 9:4

As we have therefore opportunity, let us do good unto all
men, especially unto them who are of the household of
faith.
GALATIANS 6:10

Now unto him that is able to do exceeding abundantly
above all that we ask or think, according to the power
that worketh in us.
EPHESIANS 3:20

And we desire that every one of you do shew the same
diligence to the full assurance of hope unto the end.
HEBREWS 6:11

If any of you lack wisdom, let him ask of God, that giveth
to all men liberally, and upbraideth not; and it shall be
given him.
JAMES 1:5

I can do all things through Christ which strengtheneth me.

PHILIPPIANS 4:13

Wherefore, beloved, seeing that ye look for such things, be diligent that ye may be found of him in peace, without spot, and blameless.
2 PETER 3:14

I know thy works: behold, I have set before thee an open door, and no man can shut it: for thou hast a little strength, and hast kept my word, and hast not denied my name.
REVELATION 3:8

An Honest Mother

Now therefore, if ye will obey my voice indeed, and keep
my covenant, then ye shall be a peculiar treasure unto me
above all people: for all the earth is mine.

EXODUS 19:5

And if thou wilt walk in my ways, to keep my statutes
and my commandments, as thy father David did walk,
then I will lengthen thy days.

1 KINGS 3:14

And the Lord said unto Satan, Hast thou considered my
servant Job, that there is none like him in the earth, a
perfect and an upright man, one that feareth God, and
escheweth evil? and still he holdeth fast his integrity,
although thou movedst me against him, to destroy him
without cause.

JOB 2:3

Blessed is the man that walketh not in the counsel of the
ungodly, nor standeth in the way of sinners, nor sitteth
in the seat of the scornful.
But his delight is in the law of the Lord; and in his law
doth he meditate day and night.
PSALM 1:1-2

All the paths of the Lord are mercy and truth unto such
as keep his covenant and his testimonies.
PSALM 25:10

The fear of the Lord is the beginning of wisdom: a good
understanding have all they that do his commandments:
his praise endureth for ever.
PSALM 111:10

Blessed are they that keep his testimonies, and that seek
him with the whole heart.
Thou hast commanded us to keep thy precepts diligently.
PSALM 119:2,4

Judge me, O Lord; for I have walked in mine integrity : I
have trusted also in the Lord; therefore I shall not slide.
PSALM 26:1

And as for me, thou upholdest me in mine integrity, and
settest me before thy face for ever.
PSALM 41:12

So he fed them according to the integrity of his heart;
and guided them by the skilfulness of his hands.
PSALM 78:72

The integrity of the upright shall guide them: but the
perverseness of transgressors shall destroy them.
PROVERBS 11:3

Better is the poor that walketh in his integrity, than he
that is perverse in his lips, and is a fool.
He that keepeth the commandment keepeth his own soul;
but he that despiseth his ways shall die.
PROVERBS 19:1,16

If ye be willing and obedient, ye shall eat the good of the
land.
ISAIAH 1:19

Recompense to no man evil for evil. Provide things honest
in the sight of all men.
ROMANS 12:17

The just man walketh in his integrity: his children are blessed after him.

PROVERBS 20:7

Finally, brethren, whatsoever things are true, whatsoever things are honest, whatsoever things are just, whatsoever things are pure, whatsoever things are lovely, whatsoever things are of good report; if there be any virtue, and if there be any praise, think on these things.

PHILIPPIANS 4:8

Having your conversation honest among the Gentiles: that, whereas they speak against you as evildoers, they may by your good works, which they shall behold, glorify God in the day of visitation.

1 PETER 2:12

An Understanding Mother

WHEN YOU WANT TO BE . . .

As for God, his way is perfect: the word of the Lord is tried: he is a buckler to all those that trust in him. Teach me thy way, O Lord, and lead me in a plain path, because of mine enemies.

PSALM 27:11

I am thy servant; give me understanding, that I may know thy testimonies.

The entrance of thy words giveth light; it giveth understanding unto the simple.

Let my cry come near before thee, O Lord: give me understanding according to thy word.

PSALM 119:125,130,169

Counsel is mine, and sound wisdom: I am understanding;
I have strength.
PROVERBS 8:14

Understanding is a wellspring of life unto him that hath
it: but the instruction of fools is folly.
The heart of the wise teacheth his mouth, and addeth
learning to his lips.
PROVERBS 16:22-23

Through wisdom is an house builded; and by understanding it is established:
And by knowledge shall the chambers be filled with all
precious and pleasant riches.
PROVERBS 24:3-4

For my thoughts are not your thoughts, neither are your
ways my ways, saith the Lord.
For as the heavens are higher than the earth, so are my
ways higher than your ways, and my thoughts than your
thoughts.
ISAIAH 55:8-9

Call unto me, and I will answer thee, and shew thee great
and mighty things, which thou knowest not.
JEREMIAH 33:3

Then opened he their understanding, that they might
understand the scriptures.
LUKE 24:45

For the law of the Spirit of life in Christ Jesus hath made
me free from the law of sin and death.
ROMANS 8:2

Wherefore be ye not unwise, but understanding what the
will of the Lord is.
EPHESIANS 5:17

And we know that the Son of God is come, and hath given
us an understanding, that we may know him that is true,
and we are in him that is true, even in his Son Jesus Christ.
This is the true God, and eternal life.
1 JOHN 5:20

That the God of our Lord Jesus Christ, the Father of
glory, may give unto you the spirit of wisdom and revelation in the knowledge of him:
The eyes of your understanding being enlightened; that
ye may know what is the hope of his calling, and what
the riches of the glory of his inheritance in the saints.
EPHESIANS 1:17-18

Trust in the Lord with all thine heart; and lean not unto thine own understanding.

In all thy ways acknowledge him, and he shall direct thy paths.

PROVERBS 3:5-6

A Creative Mother

Now therefore go, and I will be with thy mouth, and teach
thee what thou shalt say.
EXODUS 4:12

Only be thou strong and very courageous, that thou mayest
observe to do according to all the law, which Moses my
servant commanded thee: turn not from it to the right
hand or to the left, that thou mayest prosper whithersoever
thou goest.
JOSHUA 1:7

But there is a spirit in man: and the inspiration of the
Almighty giveth them understanding.
JOB 32:8

Then he openeth the ears of men, and sealeth their
instruction.
JOB 33:16

I will bless the Lord, who hath given me counsel: my reins
also instruct me in the night seasons.
PSALM 16:7

I will instruct thee and teach thee in the way which thou
shalt go: I will guide thee with mine eye.
PSALM 32:8

The Lord will perfect that which concerneth me: thy
mercy, O Lord, endureth for ever: forsake not the works
of thine own hands.
PSALM 138:8

A wise man will hear, and will increase learning; and a
man of understanding shall attain unto wise counsels.
PROVERBS 1:5

Wisdom is the principal thing; therefore get wisdom: and
with all thy getting get understanding.
Exalt her, and she shall promote thee: she shall bring thee
to honour, when thou dost embrace her.
PROVERBS 4:7-8

I love them that love me; and those that seek me early
shall find me. Riches and honour are with me; yea, durable
riches and righteousness.
PROVERBS 8:17-18

That I may cause those that love me to inherit substance;
and I will fill their treasures.
PROVERBS 8:21

Behold, the former things are come to pass, and new things
do I declare: before they spring forth I tell you of them.
ISAIAH 42:9

So shall the knowledge of wisdom be unto thy soul: when thou hast found it, then there shall be a reward, and thy expectation shall not be cut off.
PROVERBS 24:14

Behold, I will do a new thing; now it shall spring forth; shall ye not know it? I will even make a way in the wilderness, and rivers in the desert.
ISAIAH 43:19

Thou hast heard, see all this; and will not ye declare it? I have shewed thee new things from this time, even hidden things, and thou didst not know them.
They are created now, and not from the beginning; even before the day when thou heardest them not; lest thou shouldest say, Behold, I knew them.
ISAIAH 48:6-7

The Lord God hath given me the tongue of the learned, that I should know how to speak a word in season to him that is weary: he wakeneth morning by morning, he wakeneth mine ear to hear as the learned.
ISAIAH 50:4

And the Lord answered me, and said, Write the vision, and make it plain upon tables, that he may run that readeth it. For the vision is yet for an appointed time, but at the end it shall speak, and not lie: though it tarry, wait for it; because it will surely come, it will not tarry.
HABAKKUK 2:2-3

Ask, and it shall be given you; seek, and ye shall find; knock, and it shall be opened unto you.

MATTHEW 7:7

For who hath despised the day of small things? for they shall rejoice, and shall see the plummet in the hand of Zerubbabel with those seven; they are the eyes of the Lord, which run to and fro through the whole earth.
ZECHARIAH 4:10

For which of you, intending to build a tower, sitteth not down first, and counteth the cost, whether he have sufficient to finish it?
LUKE 14:28

Knowing that whatsoever good thing any man doeth, the same shall he receive of the Lord, whether he be bond or free.
EPHESIANS 6:8

A Hospitable Mother

WHEN YOU WANT TO BE . . .

Distributing to the necessity of saints; given to hospitality.
ROMANS 12:13

But a lover of hospitality, a lover of good men, sober,
just, holy, temperate.
TITUS 1:8

Use hospitality one to another without grudging.
I am a companion of all them that fear thee, and of them
that keep thy precepts.
PSALM 119:63

A friend loveth at all times.
PROVERBS 17:17A

I will not leave you comfortless: I will come to you.
JOHN 14:18

Make no friendship with an angry man; and with a furious
man thou shalt not go.
PROVERBS 22:24

For the mountains shall depart, and the hills be removed;
but my kindness shall not depart from thee, neither shall
the covenant of my peace be removed, saith the Lord that
hath mercy on thee.
ISAIAH 54:10

For whosoever shall do the will of my Father which is in
heaven, the same is my brother, and sister, and mother.
MATTHEW 12:50

And I say unto you, Ask, and it shall be given you; seek,
and ye shall find; knock, and it shall be opened unto you.
LUKE 11:9

But when thou art bidden, go and sit down in the lowest
room; that when he that bade thee cometh, he may say
unto thee, Friend, go up higher: then shalt thou have
worship in the presence of them that sit at meat with
thee.
LUKE 14:10

God is faithful, by whom ye were called unto the fellowship
of his Son Jesus Christ our Lord.
1 CORINTHIANS 1:9

This is my commandment, That ye love one another, as I have loved you. Greater love hath no man than this, that a man lay down his life for his friends.
Ye are my friends, if ye do whatsoever I command you. Henceforth I call you not servants; for the servant knoweth not what his lord doeth: but I have called you friends; for all things that I have heard of my Father I have made known unto you.
Ye have not chosen me, but I have chosen you, and ordained you, that ye should go and bring forth fruit, and that your fruit should remain: that whatsoever ye shall ask of the Father in my name, he may give it you.
JOHN 15:12-16

Let your conversation be without covetousness; and be content with such things as ye have: for he hath said, I will never leave thee, nor forsake thee.
HEBREWS 13:5

But if we walk in the light, as he is in the light, we have fellowship one with another, and the blood of Jesus Christ his Son cleanseth us from all sin.
1 JOHN 1:7

Behold, I stand at the door, and knock: if any man hear my voice, and open the door, I will come in to him, and will sup with him, and he with me.
REVELATION 3:20

A man that hath friends must shew himself friendly: and there is a friend that sticketh closer than a brother.

PROVERBS 18:24

A Courageous Mother

Be strong and of a good courage, fear not, nor be afraid of them: for the Lord thy God, he it is that doth go with thee; he will not fail thee, nor forsake thee.
DEUTERONOMY 31:6

Be strong and of a good courage: for thou shalt bring the children of Israel into the land which I sware unto them: and I will be with thee.
DEUTERONOMY 31:23B

And David said to Solomon his son, Be strong and of good courage, and do it: fear not, nor be dismayed: for the Lord God, even my God, will be with thee; he will not fail thee, nor forsake thee, until thou hast finished all the work for the service of the house of the Lord.
1 CHRONICLES 28:20

Be of good courage, and he shall strengthen your heart,
all ye that hope in the Lord.
PSALM 31:24

Counsel is mine, and sound wisdom: I am understanding;
I have strength.
PROVERBS 8:14

Strengthen ye the weak hands, and confirm the feeble
knees.
ISAIAH 35:3

Fear thou not; for I am with thee: be not dismayed; for I
am thy God: I will strengthen thee; yea, I will help thee;
yea, I will uphold thee with the right hand of my righteousness.
ISAIAH 41:10

The Lord God is my strength, and he will make my feet
like hinds' feet, and he will make me to walk upon mine
high places.
HABAKKUK 3:19

But ye shall receive power, after that the Holy Ghost is
come upon you: and ye shall be witnesses unto me both
in Jerusalem, and in all Judaea, and in Samaria, and unto
the uttermost part of the earth.
ACTS 1:8

Be ye strong therefore, and let not your hands be weak:
for your work shall be rewarded.
2 CHRONICLES 15:7

But God hath chosen the foolish things of the world to
confound the wise; and God hath chosen the weak things
of the world to confound the things which are mighty.
1 CORINTHIANS 1:27

For to one is given by the Spirit the word of wisdom; to
another the word of knowledge by the same Spirit.
1 CORINTHIANS 12:8

And God is able to make all grace abound toward you;
that ye, always having all sufficiency in all things, may
abound to every good work.
2 CORINTHIANS 9:8

Now unto him that is able to do exceeding abundantly
above all that we ask or think, according to the power
that worketh in us.
EPHESIANS 3:20

I can do all things through Christ which strengtheneth
me.
PHILIPPIANS 4:13

Be strong and of a good courage: for unto this people shalt thou divide for an inheritance the land, which I sware unto their fathers to give them.

JOSHUA 1:6

Cast not away therefore your confidence, which hath great recompence of reward.
For ye have need of patience, that, after ye have done the will of God, ye might receive the promise.
HEBREWS 10:35-36

If any of you lack wisdom, let him ask of God, that giveth to all men liberally, and upbraideth not; and it shall be given him.
JAMES 1:5

A Joyful Mother

Let the heavens be glad, and let the earth rejoice: and let
men say among the nations, The Lord reigneth.
1 CHRONICLES 16:31

Thou hast put gladness in my heart, more than in the
time that their com and their wine increased.
PSALM 4:7

But let all those that put their trust in thee rejoice: let
them ever shout for joy, because thou defendest them: let
them also that love thy name be joyful in thee.
PSALM 5:11

And these things write we unto you, that your joy may
be full.
1 JOHN 1:4

Weeping may endure for a night, but joy cometh in the
morning.
PSALM 30:5B

Delight thyself also in the Lord; and he shall give thee
the desires of thine heart.
PSALM 37:4

Blessed is the people that know the joyful sound: they
shall walk, O Lord, in the light of thy countenance.
PSALM 89:15

Make a joyful noise unto the Lord, all ye lands.
Serve the Lord with gladness: come before his presence
with singing. Know ye that the Lord he is God: it is he
that hath made us, and not we ourselves; we are his people,
and the sheep of his pasture. Enter into his gates with
thanksgiving, and into his courts with praise: be thankful
unto him, and bless his name.
PSALM 100:1-4

A merry heart maketh a cheerful countenance: but by
sorrow of the heart the spirit is broken.
PROVERBS 15:13

A merry heart doeth good like a medicine: but a broken
spirit drieth the bones.
PROVERBS 17:22

For ye shall go out with joy, and be led forth with peace: the mountains and the hills shall break forth before you into singing, and all the trees of the field shall clap their hands.
ISAIAH 55:12

Although the fig tree shall not blossom, neither shall fruit be in the vines; the labour of the olive shall fail, and the fields shall yield no meat; the flock shall be cut off from the fold, and there shall be no herd in the stalls: Yet I will rejoice in the Lord, I will joy in the God of my salvation.
HABAKKUK 3:17-18

Notwithstanding in this rejoice not, that the spirits are subject unto you; but rather rejoice, because your names are written in heaven.
LUKE 10:20

Now the God of hope fill you with all joy and peace in believing, that ye may abound in hope, through the power of the Holy Ghost.
ROMANS 15:13

But the fruit of the Spirit is love, joy, peace, long-suffering, gentleness, goodness, faith.
GALATIANS 5:22

Speaking to yourselves in psalms and hymns and spiritual songs, singing and making melody in your heart to the Lord.
EPHESIANS 5:19

They that sow in tears shall reap in joy.

PSALM 126:5

A Consistent Mother

WHEN YOU WANT TO BE . . .

Moreover I will establish his kingdom for ever, if he be constant to do my commandments and my judgments, as at this day.

1 CHRONICLES 28:7

But thou, O Lord, art a shield for me; my glory, and the lifter up of mine head.

PSALM 3:3

For the Lord God will help me; therefore shall I not be confounded.

ISAIAH 50:7A

Trust in the Lord with all thine heart; and lean not unto thine own understanding. In all thy ways acknowledge him, and he shall direct thy paths.
PSALM 3:5-6

For the Lord shall be thy confidence, and shall keep thy foot from being taken.
PROVERBS 3:26

He giveth power to the faint; and to them that have no might he increaseth strength.
ISAIAH 40:29

If any man serve me, let him follow me; and where I am, there shall also my servant be: if any man serve me, him will my Father honour.
JOHN 12:26

Charity never faileth: but whether there be prophecies, they shall fail; whether there be tongues, they shall cease; whether there be knowledge, it shall vanish away.
1 CORINTHIANS 13:8

If any of you lack wisdom, let him ask of God, that giveth to all men liberally, and upbraideth not; and it shall be given him.
JAMES 1:5

A man's heart deviseth his way: but the Lord directeth
his steps.
PROVERBS 16:9

It is better to trust in the Lord than to put confidence in
man.
PSALM 118:8

The Lord is my light and my salvation; whom shall I fear?
the Lord is the strength of my life; of whom shall I be
afraid?
Though an host should encamp against me, my heart shall
not fear: though war should rise against me, in this will
I be confident.
For in the time of trouble he shall hide me in his pavilion:
in the secret of his tabernacle shall he hide me; he shall
set me up upon a rock.
PSALM 27:1,3,5

For I am the Lord, I change not.
MALACHI 3:6A

Jesus Christ the same yesterday, and today, and forever.

HEBREWS 13:8

A Good Listener as a Mother

A wise man will hear, and will increase learning; and a
man of understanding shall attain unto wise counsels:
To understand a proverb, and the interpretation; the words
of the wise, and their dark sayings.
The fear of the Lord is the beginning of knowledge: but
fools despise wisdom and instruction.
My son, hear the instruction of thy father, and forsake
not the law of thy mother.
PROVERBS 1:5-8

The heart of the prudent getteth knowledge; and the ear
of the wise seeketh knowledge.
PROVERBS 18:15

And the man said unto me, Son of man, behold with thine
eyes, and hear with thine ears, and set thine heart upon
all that I shall shew thee.
EZEKIEL 40:4A

And every one that heareth these sayings of mine, and doeth them not, shall be likened unto a foolish man, which built his house upon the sand:
And the rain descended, and the floods came, and the winds blew, and beat upon that house; and it fell: and great was the fall of it.
MATTHEW 7:26-27

But blessed are your eyes, for they see: and your ears, for they hear.
MATTHEW 13:16

Take heed therefore how ye hear: for whosoever hath, to him shall be given; and whosoever hath not, from him shall be taken even that which he seemeth to have.
LUKE 8:18

He that heareth you heareth me; and he that despiseth you despiseth me; and he that despiseth me despiseth him that sent me.
LUKE 10:16

He that is of God heareth God's words: ye therefore hear them not, because ye are not of God.
JOHN 8:47

Wherefore hear the word of the Lord, ye scornful men,
that rule this people which is in Jerusalem.
ISAIAH 28:14

Pilate therefore said unto him, Art thou a king then? Jesus
answered, Thou sayest that I am a king. To this end was
I born, and for this cause came I into the world, that I
should bear witness unto the truth. Every one that is of
the truth heareth my voice.
JOHN 18:37

But be ye doers of the word, and not hearers only, deceiv-
ing your own selves. For if any be a hearer of the word,
and not a doer, he is like unto a man beholding his natural
face in a glass.
JAMES 1:23

But whoso looketh into the perfect law of liberty, and
continueth therein, he being not a forgetful hearer, but a
doer of the work, this man shall be blessed in his deed.
JAMES 1:25

He that hath an ear, let him hear what the Spirit saith
unto the churches.
REVELATION 2:29

Wherefore, my beloved brethren, let every man be swift to hear, slow to speak, slow to wrath . . .

JAMES 1:19

A Compassionate Mother

WHEN YOU WANT TO BE . . .

Then shalt thou call, and the Lord shall answer; thou shalt
cry, and he shall say, Here I am. If thou take away from
the midst of thee the yoke, the putting forth of the finger,
and speaking vanity;
And if thou draw out thy soul to the hungry, and satisfy
the afflicted soul; then shall thy light rise in obscurity,
and thy darkness be as the noon day:
And the Lord shall guide thee continually, and satisfy thy
soul in drought, and make fat thy bones: and thou shalt
be like a watered garden, and like a spring of water, whose
waters fail not.
ISAIAH 58:9-11

The Lord is my shepherd; I shall not want.
PSALM 23:1

All the paths of the Lord are mercy and truth unto such
as keep his covenant and his testimonies.
PSALM 25:10

The wicked borroweth, and payeth not again: but the
righteous sheweth mercy, and giveth.
PSALM 37:21

But he, being full of compassion, forgave their iniquity,
and destroyed them not: yea, many a time turned he his
anger away, and did not stir up all his wrath.
PSALM 78:38

He that followeth after righteousness and mercy findeth
life, righteousness, and honour.
PROVERBS 21:21

He that covereth his sins shall not prosper: but whoso
confesseth and forsaketh them shall have mercy.
PROVERBS 28:13

Can a woman forget her sucking child, that she should
not have compassion on the son of her womb? yea, they
may forget, yet will I not forget thee.
ISAIAH 49:15

And it shall come to pass, after that I have plucked them
out I will return, and have compassion on them, and will
bring them again, every man to his heritage, and every
man to his land.
JEREMIAH 12:15

And Jesus, when he came out, saw much people, and was moved with compassion toward them, because they were as sheep not having a shepherd: and he began to teach them many things.

MARK 6:34

Now when he came nigh to the gate of the city, behold, there was a dead man carried out, the only son of his mother, and she was a widow: and much people of the city was with her.
And when the Lord saw her, he had compassion on her, and said unto her, Weep not.

LUKE 7:12-13

Charity suffereth long, and is kind; charity envieth not; charity vaunteth not itself, is not puffed up,
Doth not behave itself unseemly, seeketh not her own, is not easily provoked, thinketh no evil;
Rejoiceth not in iniquity, but rejoiceth in the truth;
Beareth all things, believeth all things, hopeth all things, endureth all things.

1 CORINTHIANS 13:4-7

Finally, be ye all of one mind, having compassion one of another, love as brethren, be pitiful, be courteous.

1 PETER 3:8

He hath made his wonderful works to be remembered: the Lord is gracious and full of compassion.

PSALM 111:4

When Your Child . . .

WHEN YOUR CHILD BECOMES
UNRULY

And Samuel said, Hath the Lord as great delight in burnt offerings and sacrifices, as in obeying the voice of the Lord? Behold, to obey is better than sacrifice, and to hearken than the fat of rams.
For rebellion is as the sin of witchcraft, and stubbornness is as iniquity and idolatry. Because thou hast rejected the word of the Lord, he hath also rejected thee from being king.
1 SAMUEL 15:22-23

The discretion of a man deferreth his anger; and it is his glory to pass over a transgression.
PROVERBS 19:11

It is an honour for a man to cease from strife: but every fool will be meddling.
PROVERBS 20:3

If the spirit of the ruler rise up against thee, leave not thy place; for yielding pacifieth great offences.
ECCLESIASTES 10:4

If ye be willing and obedient, ye shall eat the good of the land: But if ye refuse and rebel, ye shall be devoured with the sword: for the mouth of the Lord hath spoken it.
ISAIAH 1:19-20

If it be possible, as much as lieth in you, live peaceably
with all men.
ROMANS 12:18

Charity suffereth long, and is kind; charity envieth not;
charity vaunteth not itself, is not puffed up,
Doth not behave itself unseemly, seeketh not her own, is
not easily provoked, thinketh no evil;
Rejoiceth not in iniquity, but rejoiceth in the truth;
Beareth all things, believeth all things, hopeth all things,
endureth all things.
1 CORINTHIANS 13:4-7

Now we exhort you, brethren, warn them that are unruly.
1 THESSALONIANS 5:14A

And the servant of the Lord must not strive; but be gentle
unto all men, apt to teach, patient.
2 TIMOTHY 2:24

To speak evil of no man, to be no brawlers, but gentle,
shewing all meekness unto all men.
TITUS 3:2

Follow peace with all men, and holiness, without which
no man shall see the Lord.
HEBREWS 12:14

Blessed are the peacemakers: for they shall be called the children of God.

MATTHEW 5:9

And the fruit of righteousness is sown in peace of them
that make peace.
JAMES 3:18

Likewise, ye younger, submit yourselves unto the elder.
Yea, all of you be subject one to another, and be clothed
with humility: for God resisteth the proud, and giveth
grace to the humble.
Humble yourselves therefore under the mighty hand of
God, that he may exalt you in due time.
1 PETER 5:5-6

Becomes Sick

WHEN YOUR CHILD . . .

And the Lord will take away from thee all sickness, and will put none of the evil diseases of Egypt, which thou knowest, upon thee; but will lay them upon all them that hate thee.
DEUTERONOMY 7:15

Bless the Lord, O my soul, and forget not all his benefits: Who forgiveth all thine iniquities; who healeth all thy diseases.
PSALM 103:2-3

My son, attend to my words; incline thine ear unto my sayings. Let them not depart from thine eyes; keep them in the midst of thine heart. For they are life unto those that find them, and health to all their flesh.
PROVERBS 4:20-22

Beloved, I wish above all things that thou mayest prosper and be in health, even as thy soul prospereth.
3 JOHN 2

Surely he hath borne our griefs, and carried our sorrows: yet we did esteem him stricken, smitten of God, and afflicted. But he was wounded for our transgressions, he was bruised for our iniquities: the chastisement of our peace was upon him; and with his stripes we are healed.
ISAIAH 53:4-5

Heal me, O Lord, and I shall be healed; save me, and I shall be saved: for thou art my praise.
JEREMIAH 17:14

For I will restore health unto thee, and I will heal thee of thy wounds, saith the Lord.
JEREMIAH 30:17A

And Jesus saith unto him, I will come and heal him.
MATTHEW 8:7

Jesus Christ the same yesterday, and to day, and for ever.
HEBREWS 13:8

Is any among you afflicted? let him pray. Is any merry? let him sing psalms. Is any sick among you? let him call for the elders of the church; and let them pray over him, anointing him with oil in the name of the Lord:
And the prayer of faith shall save the sick, and the Lord shall raise him up; and if he have committed sins, they shall be forgiven him. Confess your faults one to another, and pray one for another, that ye may be healed. The effectual fervent prayer of a righteous man availeth much.
JAMES 5:13-16

Becomes Rebellious Towards You

Train up a child in the way he should go: and when he is old, he will not depart from it.
PROVERBS 22:6

Now therefore go, and I will be with thy mouth, and teach thee what thou shalt say.
EXODUS 4:12

Teach me, and I will hold my tongue: and cause me to understand wherein I have erred.
JOB 6:24

Shew me thy ways, O Lord; teach me thy paths. What man is he that feareth the Lord? him shall he teach in the way that he shall choose.
PSALM 25:4,12

The Lord is my strength and my shield; my heart trusted in him, and I am helped: therefore my heart greatly rejoiceth; and with my song will I praise him.
PSALM 28:7

Cast thy burden upon the Lord, and he shall sustain thee:
he shall never suffer the righteous to be moved.
PSALM 55:22

Though I walk in the midst of trouble, thou wilt revive
me: thou shalt stretch forth thine hand against the wrath
of mine enemies, and thy right hand shall save me.
PSALM 138:7

Teach me to do thy will; for thou art my God: thy spirit
is good; lead me into the land of uprightness.
PSALM 143:10

Answer not a fool according to his folly, lest thou also be
like unto him.
PROVERBS 26:4

If ye be willing and obedient, ye shall eat the good of the
land: But if ye refuse and rebel, ye shall be devoured with
the sword: for the mouth of the Lord hath spoken it.
ISAIAH 1:19-20

Can a woman forget her sucking child, that she should
not have compassion on the son of her womb? yea, they
may forget, yet will I not forget thee.
ISAIAH 49:15

And I will give unto thee the keys of the kingdom of
heaven: and whatsoever thou shalt bind on earth shall be
bound in heaven: and whatsoever thou shalt loose on earth
shall be loosed in heaven.
MATTHEW 16:19

Behold, I give unto you power to tread on serpents and
scorpions, and over all the power of the enemy: and nothing shall by any means hurt you.
LUKE 10:19

Take heed to yourselves: If thy brother trespass against
thee, rebuke him; and if he repent, forgive him.
LUKE 17:3

Servants, be obedient to them that are your masters
according to the flesh, with fear and trembling, in singleness of your heart, as unto Christ;
With good will doing service, as to the Lord, and not to
men.
EPHESIANS 6:5,7

Wherefore gird up the loins of your mind, be sober, and
hope to the end for the grace that is to be brought unto
you at the revelation of Jesus Christ;
As obedient children, not fashioning yourselves according
to the former lusts in your ignorance.
1 PETER 1:13-14

Then Peter and the other apostles answered and said, We ought to obey God rather than men.

ACTS 5:29

Submit yourselves to every ordinance of man for the
Lord's sake: whether it be to the king, as supreme;
Or unto governors, as unto them that are sent by him for
the punishment of evildoers, and for the praise of them
that do well.
For so is the will of God, that with well doing ye may put
to silence the ignorance of foolish men.
1 PETER 2:13-15

Becomes Rebellious Towards God

Train up a child in the way he should go: and when he is
old, he will not depart from it.
PROVERBS 22:6

Wait on the Lord: be of good courage, and he shall
strengthen thine heart: wait, I say, on the Lord.
PSALM 27:14

Our soul waiteth for the Lord: he is our help and our
shield.
PSALM 33:20

Delight thyself also in the Lord; and he shall give thee
the desires of thine heart.
Commit thy way unto the Lord; trust also in him; and he
shall bring it to pass.
PSALM 37:4-5

Cast thy burden upon the Lord, and he shall sustain thee:
he shall never suffer the righteous to be moved.
PSALM 55:22

For the Lord will not cast off his people, neither will he
forsake his inheritance.
PSALM 94:14

I wait for the Lord, my soul doth wait, and in his word
do I hope.
PSALM 130:5

The Lord will perfect that which concerneth me: thy
mercy, O Lord, endureth for ever: forsake not the works
of thine own hands.
PSALM 138:8

Correct thy son, and he shall give thee rest; yea, he shall
give delight unto thy soul.
PROVERBS 29:17

Fear thou not; for I am with thee: be not dismayed; for I
am thy God: I will strengthen thee; yea, I will help thee;
yea, I will uphold thee with the right hand of my righteousness.
ISAIAH 41:10

And all thy children shall be taught of the Lord; and great
shall be the peace of thy children.
ISAIAH 54:13

For we walk by faith, not by sight.
2 CORINTHIANS 5:7

Let us hold fast the profession of our faith without
wavering; for he is faithful that promised.
HEBREWS 10:23

Now faith is the substance of things hoped for, the evidence
of things not seen.
But without faith it is impossible to please him: for he that
cometh to God must believe that he is, and that he is a
rewarder of them that diligently seek him.
HEBREWS 11:1,6

That the trial of your faith, being much more precious
than of gold that perisheth, though it be tried with fire,
might be found unto praise and honour and glory at the
appearing of Jesus Christ:
1 PETER 1:7

But ye are a chosen generation, a royal priesthood, an
holy nation, a peculiar people; that ye should shew forth
the praises of him who hath called you out of darkness
into his marvellous light.
1 PETER 2:9

Casting all your care upon him; for he careth for you.
1 PETER 5:7

I wait for the Lord, my soul doth wait, and in his word do I hope.

PSALM 130:5

Becomes Quarrelsome

WHEN YOUR CHILD . . .

I had fainted, unless I had believed to see the goodness
of the Lord in the land of the living.
PSALM 27:13

Commit thy way unto the Lord; trust also in him; and he
shall bring it to pass.
PSALM 37:5

Trust in the Lord with all thine heart; and lean not unto
thine own understanding.
PROVERBS 3:5

Correct thy son, and he shall give thee rest; yea, he shall
give delight unto thy soul.
PROVERBS 29:17

And they said, Believe on the Lord Jesus Christ, and thou
shalt be saved, and thy house.
ACTS 16:31

For the Lord God will help me; therefore shall I not be confounded: therefore have I set my face like a flint, and I know that I shall not be ashamed.
ISAIAH 50:7

Behold, I give unto you power to tread on serpents and scorpions, and over all the power of the enemy: and nothing shall by any means hurt you.
LUKE 10:19

So likewise, whosoever he be of you that forsaketh not all that he hath, he cannot be my disciple.
LUKE 14:33

Peace I leave with you, my peace I give unto you: not as the world giveth, give I unto you. Let not your heart be troubled, neither let it be afraid.
JOHN 14:27

Let all bitterness, and wrath, and anger, and clamour, and evil speaking, be put away from you, with all malice: And be ye kind one to another, tenderhearted, forgiving one another, even as God for Christ's sake hath forgiven you.
EPHESIANS 4:31-32

And, ye fathers, provoke not your children to wrath: but bring them up in the nurture and admonition of the Lord.
EPHESIANS 6:4

For God hath not given us the spirit of fear; but of power, and of love, and of a sound mind.
2 TIMOTHY 1:7

Pursues Unwholesome Relationships

WHEN YOUR CHILD . . .

I am a companion of all them that fear thee, and of them
that keep thy precepts.
PSALM 119:63

That thou mayest walk in the way of good men, and keep
the paths of the righteous.
PROVERBS 2:20

In all thy ways acknowledge him, and he shall direct thy
paths.
PROVERBS 3:6

The righteousness of the perfect shall direct his way: but
the wicked shall fall by his own wickedness.
PROVERBS 11:5

He that walketh with wise men shall be wise: but a
companion of fools shall be destroyed.
PROVERBS 13:20

A man that hath friends must shew himself friendly: and
there is a friend that sticketh closer than a brother.
PROVERBS 18:24

Make no friendship with an angry man; and with a furious
man thou shalt not go:
Lest thou learn his ways, and get a snare to thy soul.
PROVERBS 22:24-25

Faithful are the wounds of a friend; but the kisses of an
enemy are deceitful.
Ointment and perfume rejoice the heart: so doth the
sweetness of a man's friend by hearty counsel.
Thine own friend, and thy father's friend, forsake not;
neither go into thy brother's house in the day of thy
calamity: for better is a neighbour that is near than a
brother far off.
PROVERBS 27:6,9-10

For the mountains shall depart, and the hills be removed;
but my kindness shall not depart from thee, neither shall
the covenant of my peace be removed, saith the Lord that
hath mercy on thee.
And all thy children shall be taught of the Lord; and great
shall be the peace of thy children.
ISAIAH 54:10,13

A friend loveth at all times, and a brother is born for
adversity.
PROVERBS 17:17

This is my commandment, That ye love one another, as I have
loved you. Greater love hath no man than this, that a man lay
down his life for his friends.
Ye are my friends, if ye do whatsoever I command you.
Henceforth I call you not servants; for the servant knoweth
not what his lord doeth: but I have called you friends; for
all things that I have heard of my Father I have made
known unto you.
Ye have not chosen me, but I have chosen you, and ordained
you, that ye should go and bring forth fruit, and that your
fruit should remain: that whatsoever ye shall ask of the
Father in my name, he may give it you.
JOHN 15:12-16

But now I have written unto you not to keep company, if
any man that is called a brother be a fornicator, or cov-
etous, or an idolater, or a railer, or a drunkard, or an
extortioner; with such an one no not to eat.
1 CORINTHIANS 5:11

Be ye not unequally yoked together with unbelievers: for
what fellowship hath righteousness with unrighteousness?
and what communion hath light with darkness?
2 CORINTHIANS 6:14

Lay hands suddenly on no man, neither be partaker of
other men's sins: keep thyself pure.
1 TIMOTHY 5:22

Let no corrupt communication proceed out of your mouth, but that which is good to the use of edifying, that it may minister grace unto the hearers.

Lacks a Sense of Worth

So God created man in his own image, in the image of
God created he him; male and female created he them.
GENESIS 1:27

But thou, O Lord, art a shield for me; my glory, and the
lifter up of mine head.
PSALM 3:3

I will not be afraid of ten thousands of people, that have
set themselves against me round about.
PSALM 3:6

The Lord is my light and my salvation; whom shall I fear?
the Lord is the strength of my life; of whom shall I be
afraid?
Though an host should encamp against me, my heart shall
not fear: though war should rise against me, in this will
I be confident.
For in the time of trouble he shall hide me in his pavilion:
in the secret of his tabernacle shall he hide me; he shall
set me up upon a rock.
PSALM 27:1,3,5

It is better to trust in the Lord than to put confidence in
man.
PSALM 118:8

I will praise thee; for I am fearfully and wonderfully made:
marvellous are thy works; and that my soul knoweth right
well.
PSALM 139:14

For the Lord shall be thy confidence, and shall keep thy
foot from being taken.
PROVERBS 3:26

But now thus saith the Lord that created thee,
Jacob, and he that formed thee, O Israel, Fear not: for I
have redeemed thee, I have called thee by thy name; thou
art mine.
Even every one that is called by my name: for
have created him for my glory, I have formed him; yea, I
have made him.
This people have I formed for myself; they shall shew
forth my praise.
ISAIAH 43:1,7,21

Thus saith the Lord, thy redeemer, and he that formed
thee from the womb, I am the Lord that maketh all things;
that stretcheth forth the heavens alone; that spreadeth
abroad the earth by myself.
ISAIAH 44:24

Before I formed thee in the belly I knew thee; and before
thou earnest forth out of the womb I sanctified thee, and
I ordained thee a prophet unto the nations.
JEREMIAH 1:5

In the fear of the Lord is strong confidence: and his
children shall have a place of refuge.
PROVERBS 14:26

And changed the glory of the uncorruptible God into an
image made like to corruptible man, and to birds, and
four-footed beasts, and creeping things.
ROMANS 1:23

For who hath known the mind of the Lord, that he may
instruct him? But we have the mind of Christ.
1 CORINTHIANS 2:16

In whom the god of this world hath blinded the minds
of them which believe not, lest the light of the glorious
gospel of Christ, who is the image of God, should shine
unto them.
2 CORINTHIANS 4:4

Being confident of this very thing, that he which hath
begun a good work in you will perform it until the day
of Jesus Christ.
PHILIPPIANS 1:6

Let nothing be done through strife or vainglory; but in
lowliness of mind let each esteem other better than themselves. Look not every man on his own things, but every
man also on the things of others. Let this mind be in you,
which was also in Christ Jesus.
PHILIPPIANS 2:3-5

And have put on the new man, which is renewed in knowledge after the image of him that created him.

COLOSSIANS 3:10

Who is the image of the invisible God, the firstborn of
every creature.
COLOSSIANS 1:15

Ye are of God, little children, and have overcome them:
because greater is he that is in you, than he that is in the
world.
They are of the world: therefore speak they of the world,
and the world heareth them.
We are of God: he that knoweth God heareth us; he that
is not of God heareth not us. Hereby know we the spirit
of truth, and the spirit of error.
1 JOHN 4:4-6

Becomes Unforgiving Towards You

WHEN YOUR CHILD . . .

I will instruct thee and teach thee in the way which thou
shalt go: I will guide thee with mine eye.
PSALM 32:8

For he shall have judgment without mercy, that hath
shewed no mercy; and mercy rejoiceth against judgment.
JAMES 2:13

Cast thy burden upon the Lord, and he shall sustain thee:
he shall never suffer the righteous to be moved.
PSALM 55:22

Unless the Lord had been my help, my soul had almost
dwelt in silence. When I said, My foot slippeth; thy mercy,
O Lord, held me up.
PSALM 94:17-18

Great peace have they which love thy law: and nothing
shall offend them.
PSALM 119:165

Quicken me, O Lord, for thy name's sake: for thy righteousness' sake bring my soul out of trouble.
PSALM 143:11

Give instruction to a wise man, and he will be yet wiser:
teach a just man, and he will increase in learning.
PROVERBS 9:9

Open rebuke is better than secret love.
PROVERBS 27:5

For the Lord God will help me; therefore shall I not be
confounded.
ISAIAH 50:7A

There hath no temptation taken you but such as is common
to man: but God is faithful, who will not suffer you to be
tempted above that ye are able; but will with the temptation also make a way to escape, that ye may be able to bear
it.
1 CORINTHIANS 10:13

That he would grant you, according to the riches of his
glory, to be strengthened with might by his Spirit in the
inner man.
EPHESIANS 3:16

Finally, my brethren, be strong in the Lord, and in the
power of his might.
EPHESIANS 6:10

And above all these things put on charity, which is the
bond of perfectness.
And whatsoever ye do in word or deed, do all in the name
of the Lord Jesus, giving thanks to God and the Father
by him.
COLOSSIANS 3:14,17

If any of you lack wisdom, let him ask of God, that giveth
to all men liberally, and upbraideth not; and it shall be
given him.
JAMES 1:5

Beloved, think it not strange concerning the fiery trial
which is to try you, as though some strange thing happened
unto you: But rejoice, inasmuch as ye are partakers of
Christ's sufferings; that, when his glory shall be revealed,
ye may be glad also with exceeding joy.
1 PETER 4:12-13

Blessed are the merciful: for they shall obtain mercy.

MATTHEW 5:7

Begins to Withdraw from You

Commit thy works unto the Lord, and thy thoughts shall
be established.
PROVERBS 16:3

Even every one that is called by my name: for I have
created him for my glory, I have formed him; yea, I have
made him.
This people have I formed for myself; they shall shew
forth my praise.
ISAIAH 43:7,21

And he shall turn the heart of the fathers to the children,
and the heart of the children to their fathers, lest I come
and smite the earth with a curse.
MALACHI 4:6

And they that be wise shall shine as the brightness of the
firmament; and they that turn many to righteousness as
the stars for ever and ever.
DANIEL 12:3

For there is hope of a tree, if it be cut down, that it will sprout again, and that the tender branch thereof will not cease. Though the root thereof wax old in the earth, and the stock thereof die in the ground; Yet through the scent of water it will bud, and bring forth boughs like a plant.
JOB 14:7-9

Be of good courage, and he shall strengthen your heart, all ye that hope in the Lord.
PSALM 31:24

Why art thou cast down, O my soul? and why art thou disquieted within me? hope in God: for I shall yet praise him, who is the health of my countenance, and my God.
PSALM 43:5

Ye are the salt of the earth: but if the salt have lost his savour, wherewith shall it be salted?
MATTHEW 5:13A

And when ye stand praying, forgive, if ye have ought against any: that your Father also which is in heaven may forgive you your trespasses.
But if ye do not forgive, neither will your Father which is in heaven forgive your trespasses.
MARK 11:25-26

Now faith is the substance of things hoped for, the evidence of things not seen.
For by it the elders obtained a good report.
Through faith we understand that the worlds were framed by the word of God, so that things which are seen were not made of things which do appear.
HEBREWS 11:1-3

Has Thoughts of Suicide

I call heaven and earth to record this day against you, that I have set before you life and death, blessing and cursing: therefore choose life, that both thou and thy seed may live: That thou mayest love the Lord thy God, and that thou mayest obey his voice, and that thou mayest cleave unto him: for he is thy life, and the length of thy days: that thou mayest dwell in the land which the Lord sware unto thy fathers, to Abraham, to Isaac, and to Jacob, to give them.
DEUTERONOMY 30:19-20

One man of you shall chase a thousand: for the Lord your God, he it is that fighteth for you, as he hath promised you.
JOSHUA 23:10

David said moreover, The Lord that delivered me out of the paw of the lion, and out of the paw of the bear, he will deliver me out of the hand of this Philistine. And Saul said unto David, Go, and the Lord be with thee.
1 SAMUEL 17:37

He will keep the feet of his saints, and the wicked shall
be silent in darkness; for by strength shall no man prevail.
1 SAMUEL 2:9

I will not be afraid of ten thousands of people, that have
set themselves against me round about.
PSALM 3:6

The Lord is my light and my salvation; whom shall I fear?
the Lord is the strength of my life; of whom shall I be
afraid?
Though an host should encamp against me, my heart shall
not fear: though war should rise against me, in this will
I be confident.
For in the time of trouble he shall hide me in his pavilion:
in the secret of his tabernacle shall he hide me; he shall
set me up upon a rock.
PSALM 27:1,3,5

Being confident of this very thing, that he which hath
begun a good work in you will perform it until the day
of Jesus Christ.
PHILIPPIANS 1:6

For the Lord shall be thy confidence, and shall keep thy
foot from being taken.
PROVERBS 3:26

In the fear of the Lord is strong confidence: and his
children shall have a place of refuge.
PROVERBS 14:26

But they that wait upon the Lord shall renew their
strength; they shall mount up with wings as eagles; they
shall run, and not be weary; and they shall walk, and not
faint.
ISAIAH 40:31

But now thus saith the Lord that created thee, O Jacob,
and he that formed thee, O Israel, Fear not: for I have
redeemed thee, I have called thee by thy name; thou art
mine.
Even every one that is called by my name: for I have
created him for my glory, I have formed him; yea, I have
made him.
This people have I formed for myself; they shall shew
forth my praise.
ISAIAH 43:1,7,21

For God so loved the world, that he gave his only begotten
Son, that whosoever believeth in him should not perish,
but have everlasting life.
JOHN 3:16

For who hath known the mind of the Lord, that he may instruct him? But we have the mind of Christ.

1 CORINTHIANS 2:16

I am the door: by me if any man enter in, he shall be saved, and shall go in and out, and find pasture.
The thief cometh not, but for to steal, and to kill, and to destroy: I am come that they might have life, and that they might have it more abundantly.

JOHN 10:9-10

In whom the god of this world hath blinded the minds of them which believe not, lest the light of the glorious gospel of Christ, who is the image of God, should shine unto them.

2 CORINTHIANS 4:4

Ye are of God, little children, and have overcome them:
because greater is he that is in you, than he that is in the
world. They are of the world: therefore speak they of
the world, and the world heareth them. We are of God:
he that knoweth God heareth us; he that is not of God
heareth not us. Hereby know we the spirit of truth, and
the spirit of error.
1 JOHN 4:4-6

Thy word have I hid in mine heart, that I might not sin
against thee.
PSALM 119:11

Before the mountains were settled, before the hills was I
brought forth.
PROVERBS 8:25

It is better to trust in the Lord than to put confidence in
man.
PSALM 118:8

But thou, O Lord, art a shield for me; my glory, and the
lifter up of mine head.
PSALM 3:3

It is the spirit that quickeneth; the flesh profiteth nothing: the words that I speak unto you, they are spirit, and they are life.

JOHN 6:63

Must Bear the Burden of Physical Handicap

WHEN YOUR CHILD . . .

In my distress I called upon the Lord, and cried unto my God: he heard my voice out of his temple, and my cry came before him, even into his ears.
PSALM 18:6

Weeping may endure for a night, but joy cometh in the morning.
PSALM 30:5B

Thou art my hiding place; thou shalt preserve me from trouble; thou shalt compass me about with songs of deliverance.
PSALM 32:7

Bless the Lord, O my soul, and forget not all his benefits:
Who forgiveth all thine iniquities; who healeth all thy
diseases.
PSALM 103:2-3

Let thy tender mercies come unto me, that I may live: for
thy law is my delight.
PSALM 119:77

Surely he hath borne our griefs, and carried our sorrows:
yet we did esteem him stricken, smitten of God, and
afflicted.
But he was wounded for our transgressions, he was bruised
for our iniquities: the chastisement of our peace was upon
him; and with his stripes we are healed.
ISAIAH 53:4-5

For I will restore health unto thee, and I will heal thee
of thy wounds, saith the Lord;
JEREMIAH 30:17A

Finally, brethren, whatsoever things are true, whatsoever
things are honest, whatsoever things are just, whatsoever
things are pure, whatsoever things are lovely, whatsoever
things are of good report; if there be any virtue, and if
there be any praise, think on these things.
I can do all things through Christ which strengtheneth
me.
PHILIPPIANS 4:8,13

So teach us to number our days, that we may apply our
hearts unto wisdom.
PSALM 90:12

And Jesus saith unto him, I will come and heal him.
MATTHEW 8:7

Is any among you afflicted? let him pray. Is any merry?
let him sing psalms.
Is any sick among you? let him call for the elders of the
church; and let them pray over him, anointing him with
oil in the name of the Lord:
And the prayer of faith shall save the sick, and the Lord
shall raise him up; and if he have committed sins, they
shall be forgiven him.
Confess your faults one to another, and pray one for
another, that ye may be healed. The effectual fervent
prayer of a righteous man availeth much.
JAMES 5:13-16

That the trial of your faith, being much more precious
than of gold that perisheth, though it be tried with fire,
might be found unto praise and honour and glory at the
appearing of Jesus Christ.
1 PETER 1:7

And he said unto me, My grace is sufficient for thee: for my strength is made perfect in weakness. Most gladly therefore will I rather glory in my infirmities, that the power of Christ may rest upon me.

2 CORINTHIANS 12:9

Becomes Lazy and Disinterested in Life

And whatsoever ye do, do it heartily, as to the Lord, and not unto men.
COLOSSIANS 3:23

The soul of the sluggard desireth, and hath nothing: but the soul of the diligent shall be made fat.
PROVERBS 13:4

Whatsoever thy hand findeth to do, do it with thy might; for there is no work, nor device, nor knowledge, nor wisdom, in the grave, whither thou goest.
ECCLESIASTES 9:10

Moreover as for me, God forbid that I should sin against the Lord in ceasing to pray for you: but I will teach you the good and the right way.
1 SAMUEL 12:23

And there were four leprous men at the entering in of the gate: and they said one to another, Why sit we here until we die?
2 KINGS 7:3

I will instruct thee and teach thee in the way which thou shalt go: I will guide thee with mine eye.
PSALM 32:8

Why art thou cast down, O my soul? and why art thou disquieted within me? hope in God: for I shall yet praise him, who is the health of my countenance, and my God.
PSALM 43:5

Walk in wisdom toward them that are without, redeeming the time.
COLOSSIANS 4:5

Happy is he that hath the God of Jacob for his help, whose
hope is in the Lord his God.
PSALM 146:5

Then the king, when he heard these words, was sore
displeased with himself, and set his heart on Daniel to
deliver him: and he laboured till the going down of the
sun to deliver him.
DANIEL 6:14

Let your light so shine before men, that they may see your
good works, and glorify your Father which is in heaven.
MATTHEW 5:16

Now the God of hope fill you with all joy and peace in
believing, that ye may abound in hope, through the power
of the Holy Ghost.
ROMANS 15:13

Put on the whole armour of God, that ye may be able to
stand against the wiles of the devil.
Wherefore take unto you the whole armour of God, that
ye may be able to withstand in the evil day, and having
done all, to stand.
Praying always with all prayer and supplication in the
Spirit, and watching thereunto with all perseverance and
supplication for all saints.
EPHESIANS 6:11,13,18

And the peace of God, which passeth all understanding, shall keep your hearts and minds through Christ Jesus.

PHILIPPIANS 4:7

Becomes Disillusioned Towards Religion

WHEN YOUR CHILD . . .

For thou art my rock and my fortress; therefore for thy
name's sake lead me, and guide me.
Pull me out of the net that they have laid privily for me:
for thou art my strength.
Into thine hand I commit my spirit: thou hast redeemed
me, O Lord God of truth.
PSALM 31:3-5

Thou art my hiding place; thou shalt preserve me from
trouble; thou shalt compass me about with songs of deliverance.
PSALM 32:7

Commit thy way unto the Lord; trust also in him; and he
shall bring it to pass.
And he shall bring forth thy righteousness as the light,
and thy judgment as the noonday.
Rest in the Lord, and wait patiently for him: fret not
thyself because of him who prospereth in his way, because
of the man who bringeth wicked devices to pass.
PSALM 37:5-7

For in thee, O Lord, do I hope: thou wilt hear, O Lord my
God.
PSALM 38:15

In my distress I cried unto the Lord, and he heard me.
Deliver my soul, O Lord, from lying lips, and from a
deceitful tongue.
PSALM 120:1-2

Though I walk in the midst of trouble, thou wilt revive
me: thou shalt stretch forth thine hand against the wrath
of mine enemies, and thy right hand shall save me.
PSALM 138:7

The lip of truth shall be established for ever: but a lying
tongue is but for a moment.
PROVERBS 12:19

Commit thy works unto the Lord, and thy thoughts shall
be established.
PROVERBS 16:3

Say not, I will do so to him as he hath done to me: I will
render to the man according to his work.
PROVERBS 24:29

When thou passest through the waters, I will be with thee; and through the rivers, they shall not overflow thee: when thou walkest through the fire, thou shalt not be burned; neither shall the flame kindle upon thee.
ISAIAH 43:2

And the Lord shall guide thee continually, and satisfy thy soul in drought, and make fat thy bones: and thou shalt be like a watered garden, and like a spring of water, whose waters fail not.
ISAIAH 58:11

I the Lord search the heart, I try the reins, even to give every man according to his ways, and according to the fruit of his doings.
JEREMIAH 17:10

Woe unto you, scribes and Pharisees, hypocrites! for ye are like unto whited sepulchres, which indeed appear beautiful outward, but are within full of dead men's bones, and of all uncleanness.
Even so ye also outwardly appear righteous unto men, but within ye are full of hypocrisy and iniquity.
MATTHEW 23:27-28

And who is he that will harm you, if ye be followers of that which is good?
1 PETER 3:13

The Lord is good, a strong hold in the day of trouble; and he knoweth them that trust in him.

NAHUM 1:7

And when ye stand praying, forgive, if ye have ought against any: that your Father also which is in heaven may forgive you your trespasses.
But if ye do not forgive, neither will your Father which is in heaven forgive your trespasses.

MARK 11:25-26

If any man among you seem to be religious, and bridleth not his tongue, but deceiveth his own heart, this man's religion is vain.
Pure religion and undefiled before God and the Father is this, To visit the fatherless and widows in their affliction, and to keep himself unspotted from the world.

JAMES 1:26-27

Lacks the Desire to Attend Church

Be strong and of a good courage, fear not, nor be afraid of them: for the Lord thy God, he it is that doth go with thee; he will not fail thee, nor forsake thee.
DEUTERONOMY 31:6

And if it seem evil unto you to serve the Lord, choose you this day whom ye will serve; whether the gods which your fathers served that were on the other side of the flood, or the gods of the Amorites, in whose land ye dwell: but as for me and my house, we will serve the Lord.
JOSHUA 24:15

Moreover as for me, God forbid that I should sin against the Lord in ceasing to pray for you: but I will teach you the good and the right way.
1 SAMUEL 12:23

Glory and honour are in his presence; strength and
gladness are in his place.
1 CHRONICLES 16:27

Through thee will we push down our enemies: through
thy name will we tread them under that rise up against us.
PSALM 44:5

A brother offended is harder to be won than a strong city:
and their contentions are like the bars of a castle.
PROVERBS 18:19

The spirit of the Lord God is upon me; because the Lord
hath anointed me to preach good tidings unto the meek;
he hath sent me to bind up the brokenhearted, to proclaim
liberty to the captives, and the opening of the prison to
them that are bound.
ISAIAH 61:1

And they that be wise shall shine as the brightness of the
firmament; and they that turn many to righteousness as
the stars for ever and ever.
DANIEL 12:3

Ask, and it shall be given you; seek, and ye shall find;
knock, and it shall be opened unto you:
For every one that asketh receiveth; and he that seeketh
findeth; and to him that knocketh it shall be opened.
MATTHEW 7:7-8

And ye shall know the truth, and the truth shall make you free.
If the Son therefore shall make you free, ye shall be free indeed.
JOHN 8:32,36

Verily, verily, I say unto you, He that believeth on me, the works that I do shall he do also; and greater works than these shall he do; because I go unto my Father.
JOHN 14:12

But ye shall receive power, after that the Holy Ghost is come upon you: and ye shall be witnesses unto me both in Jerusalem, and in all Judaea, and in Samaria, and unto the uttermost part of the earth.
ACTS 1:8

Wherefore he saith, Awake thou that sleepest, and arise from the dead, and Christ shall give thee light.
EPHESIANS 5:14

I can do all things through Christ which strengtheneth me.
PHILIPPIANS 4:13

Neglect not the gift that is in thee, which was given thee by prophecy, with the laying on of the hands of the presbytery.

1 TIMOTHY 4:14

Strengthened with all might, according to his glorious power, unto all patience and long-suffering with joyfulness.
COLOSSIANS 1:11

Wherefore I put thee in remembrance that thou stir up the gift of God, which is in thee by the putting on of my hands.
2 TIMOTHY 1:6

Study to shew thyself approved unto God, a workman that needeth not to be ashamed, rightly dividing the word of truth.
2 TIMOTHY 2:15

Is Heartbroken by Divorce

For the Lord thy God is a merciful God; he will not forsake thee, neither destroy thee, nor forget the covenant of thy fathers which he sware unto them.

DEUTERONOMY 4:31

Be strong and of a good courage, fear not, nor be afraid of them: for the Lord thy God, he it is that doth go with thee; he will not fail thee, nor forsake thee.

DEUTERONOMY 31:6

For the Lord will not forsake his people for his great name's sake: because it hath pleased the Lord to make you his people.

1 SAMUEL 12:22

And they that know thy name will put their trust in thee: for thou, Lord, hast not forsaken them that seek thee.

PSALM 9:10

When my father and my mother forsake me, then the Lord will take me up. Teach me thy way, O Lord, and lead me in a plain path, because of mine enemies.
PSALM 27:10-11

Weeping may endure for a night, but joy cometh in the morning.
PSALM 30:5B

I have been young, and now am old; yet have I not seen the righteous forsaken, nor his seed begging bread.
PSALM 37:25

Why art thou cast down, O my soul? and why art thou disquieted within me? hope in God: for I shall yet praise him, who is the health of my countenance, and my God.
PSALM 43:5

Because he hath set his love upon me, therefore will I deliver him: I will set him on high, because he hath known my name. He shall call upon me, and I will answer him: I will be with him in trouble; I will deliver him, and honour him.
PSALM 91:14-15

For the Lord will not cast off his people, neither will he forsake his inheritance.
PSALM 94:14

Persecuted, but not forsaken; cast down, but not destroyed.
2 CORINTHIANS 4:9

When the poor and needy seek water, and there is none, and their tongue faileth for thirst, I the Lord will hear them, I the God of Israel will not forsake them.
ISAIAH 41:17

Can a woman forget her sucking child, that she should not have compassion on the son of her womb? yea, they may forget, yet will I not forget thee.
Behold, I have graven thee upon the palms of my hands; thy walls are continually before me.
ISAIAH 49:15-16

Thou shalt no more be termed Forsaken; neither shall thy land any more be termed Desolate: but thou shalt be called Hephzibah, and thy land Beulah: for the Lord delighteth in thee, and thy land shall be married.
ISAIAH 62:4

The Spirit of the Lord is upon me, because he hath anointed me to preach the gospel to the poor; he hath sent me to heal the brokenhearted, to preach deliverance to the captives, and recovering of sight to the blind, to set at liberty them that are bruised,
To preach the acceptable year of the Lord.
LUKE 4:18-19

Let your conversation be without covetousness; and be content with such things as ye have: for he hath said, I will never leave thee, nor forsake thee.
HEBREWS 13:5

Casting all your care upon him; for he careth for you.
1 PETER 5:7

I will not leave you comfortless: I will come to you.

JOHN 14:18

Experiences Personal Failure or Loss

WHEN YOUR CHILD . . .

He maketh me to lie down in green pastures: he leadeth
me beside the still waters.
He restoreth my soul: he leadeth me in the paths of
righteousness for his name's sake.
PSALM 23:2-3

Shew me thy ways, O Lord; teach me thy paths.
Lead me in thy truth, and teach me: for thou art the God
of my salvation; on thee do I wait all the day.
PSALM 25:4-5

Let integrity and uprightness preserve me; for I wait on
thee.
PSALM 25:21

Wait on the Lord: be of good courage, and he shall
strengthen thine heart: wait, I say, on the Lord.
PSALM 27:14

Rest in the Lord, and wait patiently for him: fret not thyself because of him who prospereth in his way, because of the man who bringeth wicked devices to pass.
The steps of a good man are ordered by the Lord: and he delighteth in his way. Though he fall, he shall not be utterly cast down: for the Lord upholdeth him with his hand.
PSALM 37:7,23-24

Blessed is the man that heareth me, watching daily at my gates, waiting at the posts of my doors.
PROVERBS 8:34

For thus saith the Lord God, the Holy One of Israel; In returning and rest shall ye be saved; in quietness and in confidence shall be your strength: and ye would not.
ISAIAH 30:15

But they that wait upon the Lord shall renew their strength; they shall mount up with wings as eagles; they shall run, and not be weary; and they shall walk, and not faint.
ISAIAH 40:31

And he said unto them, Come ye yourselves apart into a desert place, and rest a while: for there were many coming and going, and they had no leisure so much as to eat.
MARK 6:31

Wherefore seeing we also are compassed about with so
great a cloud of witnesses, let us lay aside every weight,
and the sin which doth so easily beset us, and let us run
with patience the race that is set before us.
HEBREWS 12:1

If any of you lack wisdom, let him ask of God, that giveth
to all men liberally, and upbraideth not; and it shall be
given him.
JAMES 1:5

Who are kept by the power of God through faith unto
salvation ready to be revealed in the last time.
Wherein ye greatly rejoice, though now for a season, if
need be, ye are in heaviness through manifold temptations:
That the trial of your faith, being much more precious
than of gold that perisheth, though it be tried with fire,
might be found unto praise and honour and glory at the
appearing of Jesus Christ:
Whom having not seen, ye love; in whom, though now
ye see him not, yet believing, ye rejoice with joy unspeakable and full of glory.
1 PETER 1:5-8

Be sober, be vigilant; because your adversary the devil,
as a roaring lion, walketh about, seeking whom he may
devour: Whom resist stedfast in the faith, knowing that
the same afflictions are accomplished in your brethren
that are in the world.
1 PETER 5:8-9

Through wisdom is an house builded; and by understanding it is established: For a just man falleth seven times, and riseth up again: but the wicked shall fall into mischief.

PROVERBS 24:3,16

Possesses Exceptional Abilities

WHEN YOUR CHILD . . .

I will instruct thee and teach thee in the way which thou
shalt go: I will guide thee with mine eye.
PSALM 32:8

The Lord will perfect that which concerneth me: thy
mercy, O Lord, endureth for ever: forsake not the works
of thine own hands.
PSALM 138:8

I will praise thee; for I am fearfully and wonderfully made:
marvellous are thy works; and that my soul knoweth right
well.
PSALM 139:14

Bless the Lord, O my soul, and forget not all his benefits:
Who forgiveth all thine iniquities; who healeth all thy
diseases; Who redeemeth thy life from destruction; who
crowneth thee with lovingkindness and tender mercies.
PSALM 103:2-4

My son, attend to my words; incline thine ear unto my sayings.
PROVERBS 4:20

Counsel is mine, and sound wisdom: I am understanding;
I have strength.
PROVERBS 8:14

And thine ears shall hear a word behind thee, saying, This
is the way, walk ye in it, when ye turn to the right hand,
and when ye turn to the left.
ISAIAH 30:21

Children in whom was no blemish, but well favoured, and
skilful in all wisdom, and cunning in knowledge, and
understanding science, and such as had ability in them to
stand in the king's palace.
DANIEL 1:4A

Heal the sick, cleanse the lepers, raise the dead, cast out
devils: freely ye have received, freely give.
MATTHEW 10:8

But he that knew not, and did commit things worthy of
stripes, shall be beaten with few stripes. For unto whom-
soever much is given, of him shall be much required: and
to whom men have committed much, of him they will ask
the more.
LUKE 12:48

Therefore let no man glory in men. For all things are yours;
And ye are Christ's; and Christ is God's.
1 CORINTHIANS 3:21,23

And if ye be Christ's, then are ye Abraham's seed, and
heirs according to the promise.
GALATIANS 3:29

All scripture is given by inspiration of God, and is
profitable for doctrine, for reproof, for correction, for
instruction in righteousness: That the man of God may
be perfect, throughly furnished unto all good works.
2 TIMOTHY 3:16-17

Is Beyond Your Daily Influence

WHEN YOUR CHILD . . .

The Lord lift up his countenance upon thee, and give thee
peace.
NUMBERS 6:26

For the Lord thy God is a merciful God; he will not forsake
thee, neither destroy thee, nor forget the covenant of thy
fathers which he sware unto them.
DEUTERONOMY 4:31

Be strong and of a good courage, fear not, nor be afraid
of them: for the Lord thy God, he it is that doth go with
thee; he will not fail thee, nor forsake thee.
And the Lord, he it is that doth go before thee; he will be
with thee, he will not fail thee, neither forsake thee: fear
not, neither be dismayed.
DEUTERONOMY 31:6,8

Wait on the Lord: be of good courage, and he shall
strengthen thine heart: wait, I say, on the Lord.
PSALM 27:14

Delight thyself also in the Lord; and he shall give thee
the desires of thine heart.
I have been young, and now am old; yet have I not seen
the righteous forsaken, nor his seed begging bread.
PSALM 37:4,25

Lo, children are an heritage of the Lord: and the fruit of
the womb is his reward. As arrows are in the hand of a
mighty man; so are children of the youth. Happy is the
man that hath his quiver full of them: they shall not be
ashamed.
PSALM 127:3-5A

A man's heart deviseth his way: but the Lord directeth
his steps.
PROVERBS 16:9

The father of the righteous shall greatly rejoice: and he
that begetteth a wise child shall have joy of him.
PROVERBS 23:24

Correct thy son, and he shall give thee rest; yea, he shall
give delight unto thy soul.
PROVERBS 29:17

Can a woman forget her sucking child, that she should not have compassion on the son of her womb? yea, they may forget, yet will I not forget thee.
Behold, I have graven thee upon the palms of my hands; thy walls are continually before me.

ISAIAH 49:15-16

Teaching them to observe all things whatsoever I have commanded you: and, lo, I am with you alway, even unto the end of the world. Amen.

MATTHEW 28:20

That the trial of your faith, being much more precious than of gold that perisheth, though it be tried with fire, might be found unto praise and honour and glory at the appearing of Jesus Christ.

1 PETER 1:7

Casting all your care upon him; for he careth for you.

1 PETER 5:7

Train up a child in the way he should go: and when he is old, he will not depart from it.

PROVERBS 22:6

Departs from His/ Her Commitment to God

The eternal God is thy refuge, and underneath are the
everlasting arms: and he shall thrust out the enemy from
before thee; and shall say, Destroy them.
DEUTERONOMY 33:27

Be still, and know that I am God: I will be exalted among
the heathen, I will be exalted in the earth.
PSALM 46:10

And call upon me in the day of trouble: I will deliver thee,
and thou shalt glorify me.
PSALM 50:15

Cast thy burden upon the Lord, and he shall sustain thee:
he shall never suffer the righteous to be moved.
PSALM 55:22

He healeth the broken in heart, and bindeth up their
wounds.
PSALM 147:3

My flesh and my heart faileth: but God is the strength of
my heart, and my portion for ever.
PSALM 73:26

In the multitude of my thoughts within me thy comforts
delight my soul.
PSALM 94:19

Fear thou not; for I am with thee: be not dismayed; for I
am thy God: I will strengthen thee; yea, I will help thee;
yea, I will uphold thee with the right hand of my righteousness.
For I the Lord thy God will hold thy right hand, saying
unto thee, Fear not; I will help thee.
ISAIAH 41:10,13

I came not to call the righteous, but sinners to repentance.
LUKE 5:32

For the Son of man is come to seek and to save that which
was lost.
LUKE 19:10

In your patience possess ye your souls.
LUKE 21:19

The Lord is not slack concerning his promise, as some
men count slackness; but is long-suffering to us-ward,
not willing that any should perish, but that all should
come to repentance.
2 PETER 3:9

Neglects Regular Contact with You

WHEN YOUR CHILD . . .

I will instruct thee and teach thee in the way which thou
shalt go: I will guide thee with mine eye.
PSALM 32:8

Teach me good judgment and knowledge: for I have
believed thy commandments.
PSALM 119:66

For the Lord shall be thy confidence, and shall keep thy
foot from being taken.
PROVERBS 3:26

Can a woman forget her sucking child, that she should
not have compassion on the son of her womb? yea, they
may forget, yet will I not forget thee.
Behold, I have graven thee upon the palms of my hands;
thy walls are continually before me.
ISAIAH 49:15-16

Rejoicing in hope; patient in tribulation; continuing instant
in prayer.
ROMANS 12:12

And all thy children shall be taught of the Lord; and great
shall be the peace of thy children.
ISAIAH 54:13

Thou shalt no more be termed Forsaken; neither shall
thy land any more be termed Desolate.
ISAIAH 62:4A

Call unto me, and I will answer thee, and shew thee great
and mighty things, which thou knowest not.
JEREMIAH 33:3

Moreover if thy brother shall trespass against thee, go
and tell him his fault between thee and him alone: if he
shall hear thee, thou hast gained thy brother.
MATTHEW 18:15

Teaching them to observe all things whatsoever I have
commanded you: and, lo, I am with you alway, even unto
the end of the world. Amen.
MATTHEW 28:20

What shall we then say to these things? If God be for us,
who can be against us?
ROMANS 8:31

Now the God of hope fill you with all joy and peace in
believing, that ye may abound in hope, through the power
of the Holy Ghost.
ROMANS 15:13

Charity suffereth long, and is kind; charity envieth not;
charity vaunteth not itself, is not puffed up,
Doth not behave itself unseemly, seeketh not her own, is
not easily provoked, thinketh no evil;
Rejoiceth not in iniquity, but rejoiceth in the truth;
Beareth all things, believeth all things, hopeth all things,
endureth all things.
1 CORINTHIANS 13:4-7

Makes Mistakes That Grieve You

For the Lord thy God is a merciful God; he will not forsake
thee, neither destroy thee, nor forget the covenant of thy
fathers which he sware unto them.
DEUTERONOMY 4:31

Wait on the Lord: be of good courage, and he shall
strengthen thine heart: wait, I say, on the Lord.
PSALM 27:14

Our soul waiteth for the Lord: he is our help and our
shield.
PSALM 33:20

Cast thy burden upon the Lord, and he shall sustain thee:
he shall never suffer the righteous to be moved.
PSALM 55:22

For the Lord will not cast off his people, neither will he forsake his inheritance.
PSALM 94:14

I wait for the Lord, my soul doth wait, and in his word do I hope.
PSALM 130:5

The Lord will perfect that which concerneth me: thy mercy, O Lord, endureth for ever: forsake not the works of thine own hands.
PSALM 138:8

Fear thou not; for I am with thee: be not dismayed; for I am thy God: I will strengthen thee; yea, I will help thee; yea, I will uphold thee with the right hand of my righteousness.
ISAIAH 41:10

And we know that all things work together for good to them that love God, to them who are the called according to his purpose.
ROMANS 8:28

For we walk by faith, not by sight.
2 CORINTHIANS 5:7

Let us hold fast the profession of our faith without
wavering; for he is faithful that promised.
HEBREWS 10:23

Now faith is the substance of things hoped for, the evidence
of things not seen.
But without faith it is impossible to please him: for he that
cometh to God must believe that he is, and that he is a
rewarder of them that diligently seek him.
HEBREWS 11:1,6

That the trial of your faith, being much more precious
than of gold that perisheth, though it be tried with fire,
might be found unto praise and honour and glory at the
appearing of Jesus Christ.
1 PETER 1:7

But ye are a chosen generation, a royal priesthood, an
holy nation, a peculiar people; that ye should shew forth
the praises of him who hath called you out of darkness
into his marvelous light.
1 PETER 2:9

Casting all your care upon him; for he careth for you.

1 PETER 5:7

Blames You for His/Her Problems

Many are the afflictions of the righteous: but the Lord delivereth him out of them all.
PSALM 34:19

This thou hast seen, O Lord: keep not silence: O Lord, be not far from me.
PSALM 35:22

Cast thy burden upon the Lord, and he shall sustain thee: he shall never suffer the righteous to be moved.
PSALM 55:22

He only is my rock and my salvation; he is my defence; I shall not be greatly moved.
PSALM 62:2

The Lord will perfect that which concerneth me: thy
mercy, O Lord, endureth for ever: forsake not the works
of thine own hands.
PSALM 138:8

Trust in the Lord with all thine heart; and lean not unto
thine own understanding. In all thy ways acknowledge
him, and he shall direct thy paths.
PROVERBS 3:5-6

He that handleth a matter wisely shall find good: and
whoso trusteth in the Lord, happy is he.
PROVERBS 16:20

The fear of man bringeth a snare: but whoso putteth his
trust in the Lord shall be safe.
PROVERBS 29:25

Behold, God is my salvation; I will trust, and not be afraid:
for the Lord Jehovah is my strength and my song; he also
is become my salvation.
ISAIAH 12:2

Thou wilt keep him in perfect peace, whose mind is stayed
on thee: because he trusteth in thee. Trust ye in the Lord
for ever: for in the Lord Jehovah is everlasting strength.
ISAIAH 26:3-4

O Lord, be gracious unto us; we have waited for thee: be thou their arm every morning, our salvation also in the time of trouble.
ISAIAH 33:2

Fear thou not; for I am with thee: be not dismayed; for I am thy God: I will strengthen thee; yea, I will help thee; yea, I will uphold thee with the right hand of my righteousness.
ISAIAH 41:10

Therefore I will look unto the Lord; I will wait for the God of my salvation: my God will hear me.
MICAH 7:7

What shall we then say to these things? If God be for us, who can be against us?
ROMANS 8:31

Looking diligently lest any man fail of the grace of God; lest any root of bitterness springing up trouble you, and thereby many be defiled.
HEBREWS 12:15

Beloved, think it not strange concerning the fiery trial which is to try you, as though some strange thing happened unto you: But rejoice, inasmuch as ye are partakers of Christ's sufferings; that, when his glory shall be revealed, ye may be glad also with exceeding joy.
1 PETER 4:12-13

Be ye angry, and sin not: let not the sun go down upon your wrath: Let all bitterness, and wrath, and anger, and clamour, and evil speaking, be put away from you, with all malice.

EPHESIANS 4:26,31

Fear the Consequences of Your Child's Lifestyle

WHEN YOU . . .

I had fainted, unless I had believed to see the goodness
of the Lord in the land of the living.
PSALM 27:13

Commit thy way unto the Lord; trust also in him; and he
shall bring it to pass.
PSALM 37:5

Blessed are they that keep his testimonies, and that seek
him with the whole heart.
Thy word have I hid in mine heart, that I might not sin
against thee.
Give me understanding, and I shall keep thy law; yea, I
shall observe it with my whole heart.
Thy word is a lamp unto my feet, and a light unto my
path.
PSALM 119:2,11,34,105

Trust in the Lord with all thine heart; and lean not unto
thine own understanding.
PROVERBS 3:5

For the Lord God will help me; therefore shall I not be
confounded: therefore have I set my face like a flint, and
I know that I shall not be ashamed.
ISAIAH 50:7

And ye shall seek me, and find me, when ye shall search
for me with all your heart.
JEREMIAH 29:13

Behold, I give unto you power to tread on serpents and
scorpions, and over all the power of the enemy: and nothing shall by any means hurt you.
LUKE 10:19

So likewise, whosoever he be of you that forsaketh not
all that he hath, he cannot be my disciple.
LUKE 14:33

Peace I leave with you, my peace I give unto you: not as
the world giveth, give I unto you. Let not your heart be
troubled, neither let it be afraid.
JOHN 14:27

And they said, Believe on the Lord Jesus Christ, and thou shalt be saved, and thy house.
ACTS 16:31

Let all bitterness, and wrath, and anger, and clamour, and evil speaking, be put away from you, with all malice: And be ye kind one to another, tenderhearted, forgiving one another, even as God for Christ's sake hath forgiven you.
EPHESIANS 4:31-32

And, ye fathers, provoke not your children to wrath: but bring them up in the nurture and admonition of the Lord.
EPHESIANS 6:4

But what things were gain to me, those I counted loss for Christ.
PHILIPPIANS 3:7

For God hath not given us the spirit of fear; but of power, and of love, and of a sound mind.
2 TIMOTHY 1:7

There is no fear in love; but perfect love casteth out fear: because fear hath torment. He that feareth is not made perfect in love.
1 JOHN 4:18

Correct thy son, and he shall give thee rest; yea, he shall give delight unto thy soul.

PROVERBS 29:17

When Your Husband . . .

IS NOT COMMITTED TO CHRIST

The eternal God is thy refuge, and underneath are the everlasting arms: and he shall thrust out the enemy from before thee; and shall say, Destroy them.
DEUTERONOMY 33:27

And if it seem evil unto you to serve the Lord, choose you this day whom ye will serve.
JOSHUA 24:15A

Be still, and know that I am God: I will be exalted among the heathen, I will be exalted in the earth.
PSALM 46:10

And call upon me in the day of trouble: I will deliver thee, and thou shalt glorify me.
PSALM 50:15

Cast thy burden upon the Lord, and he shall sustain thee: he shall never suffer the righteous to be moved.
PSALM 55:22

My flesh and my heart faileth: but God is the strength of my heart, and my portion for ever.
PSALM 73:26

Thou therefore endure hardness, as a good soldier of Jesus Christ.
2 TIMOTHY 2:3

The Lord is not slack concerning his promise, as some men count slackness; but is long-suffering to us-ward, not willing that any should perish, but that all should come to repentance.
2 PETER 3:9

In the multitude of my thoughts within me thy comforts
delight my soul.
PSALM 94:19

In your patience possess ye your souls.
LUKE 21:19

He healeth the broken in heart, and bindeth up their
wounds.
PSALM 147:3

Fear thou not; for I am with thee: be not dismayed; for I
am thy God: I will strengthen thee; yea, I will help thee;
yea, I will uphold thee with the right hand of my righteousness. Behold, all they that were incensed against thee
shall be ashamed and confounded: they shall be as nothing;
and they that strive with thee shall perish.
Thou shalt seek them, and shalt not find them, even them
that contended with thee: they that war against thee shall
be as nothing, and as a thing of nought.
For I the Lord thy God will hold thy right hand, saying
unto thee, Fear not; I will help thee.
ISAIAH 41:10-13

The Lord God hath given me the tongue of the learned,
that I should know how to speak a word in season to him
that is weary: he wakeneth morning by morning, he wakeneth mine ear to hear as the learned.
ISAIAH 50:4

For verily I say unto you, That whosoever shall say unto
this mountain, Be thou removed, and be thou cast into
the sea; and shall not doubt in his heart, but shall believe
that those things which he saith shall come to pass; he
shall have whatsoever he saith.
MARK 11:23

For the Son of man is come to seek and to save that which was lost.

LUKE 19:10

For with God nothing shall be impossible.
LUKE 1:37

I came not to call the righteous, but sinners to repentance.
LUKE 5:32

Not that I speak in respect of want: for I have learned, in whatsoever state I am, therewith to be content. I know both how to be abased, and I know how to abound: every where and in all things I am instructed both to be full and to be hungry, both to abound and to suffer need. I can do all things through Christ which strengtheneth me.
PHILIPPIANS 4:11-13

Does Not Assume His Role as A Spiritual Leader

WHEN YOUR HUSBAND . . .

Now therefore go, and I will be with thy mouth, and teach
thee what thou shalt say.
EXODUS 4:12

Teach me, and I will hold my tongue: and cause me to
understand wherein I have erred.
JOB 6:24

Shew me thy ways, O Lord; teach me thy paths.
What man is he that feareth the Lord? him shall he teach
in the way that he shall choose.
PSALM 25:4,12

Teach me thy way, O Lord, and lead me in a plain path,
because of mine enemies.
PSALM 27:11

Teach me to do thy will; for thou art my God: thy spirit
is good; lead me into the land of uprightness.
Keep my commandments, and live; and my law as the
apple of thine eye.
PROVERBS 7:2

If ye be willing and obedient, ye shall eat the good of the land: But if ye refuse and rebel, ye shall be devoured with the sword: for the mouth of the Lord hath spoken it.
ISAIAH 1:19-20

Then Peter and the other apostles answered and said, We ought to obey God rather than men.
ACTS 5:29

Servants, be obedient to them that are your masters according to the flesh, with fear and trembling, in single-ness of your heart, as unto Christ;
With good will doing service, as to the Lord, and not to men.
EPHESIANS 6:5,7

Wherefore gird up the loins of your mind, be sober, and hope to the end for the grace that is to be brought unto you at the revelation of Jesus Christ;
As obedient children, not fashioning yourselves according to the former lusts in your ignorance.
1 PETER 1:13-14

Submit yourselves to every ordinance of man for the Lord's sake: whether it be to the king, as supreme;
Or unto governors, as unto them that are sent by him for the punishment of evildoers, and for the praise of them that do well. For so is the will of God, that with well doing ye may put to silence the ignorance of foolish men.
1 PETER 2:13-15

Likewise, ye wives, be in subjection to your own husbands; that, if any obey not the word, they also may without the word be won by the conversation of the wives.
1 PETER 3:1

Seems Overly Strict with the Children

WHEN YOUR HUSBAND . . .

The Lord is my light and my salvation; whom shall I fear?
the Lord is the strength of my life; of whom shall I be
afraid?
Though an host should encamp against me, my heart shall
not fear: though war should rise against me, in this will
I be confident.
Wait on the Lord: be of good courage, and he shall
strengthen thine heart: wait, I say, on the Lord.
PSALM 27:1,3,14

For thou art my rock and my fortress; therefore for thy
name's sake lead me, and guide me.
PSALM 31:3

Thou art my hiding place; thou shalt preserve me from
trouble; thou shalt compass me about with songs of deliverance. I will instruct thee and teach thee in the way
which thou shalt go: I will guide thee with mine eye.
PSALM 32:7-8

Train up a child in the way he should go: and when he is
old, he will not depart from it.
PROVERBS 22:6

Finally, brethren, whatsoever things are true, whatsoever
things are honest, whatsoever things are just, whatsoever
things are pure, whatsoever things are lovely, whatsoever
things are of good report; if there be any virtue, and if
there be any praise, think on these things.
I know both how to be abased, and I know how to abound:
every where and in all things I am instructed both to be
full and to be hungry, both to abound and to suffer need.
I can do all things through Christ which strengtheneth
me.
PHILIPPIANS 4:8,12-13

For we know him that hath said, Vengeance belongeth
unto me, I will recompense, saith the Lord. And again,
The Lord shall judge his people.
HEBREWS 10:30

Forbearing one another, and forgiving one another, if any
man have a quarrel against any: even as Christ forgave
you, so also do ye. And above all these things put on
charity, which is the bond of perfectness.
Fathers, provoke not your children to anger, lest they be
discouraged.
COLOSSIANS 3:13-14,21

If any of you lack wisdom, let him ask of God, that giveth
to all men liberally, and upbraideth not; and it shall be
given him.
JAMES 1:5

But if ye have bitter envying and strife in your hearts,
glory not, and lie not against the truth.
For where envying and strife is, there is confusion and
every evil work.
But the wisdom that is from above is first pure, then
peaceable, gentle, and easy to be entreated, full of mercy
and good fruits, without partiality, and without hypocrisy.
And the fruit of righteousness is sown in peace of them
that make peace.
JAMES 3:14,16-18

Confess your faults one to another, and pray one for
another, that ye may be healed. The effectual fervent
prayer of a righteous man availeth much.
JAMES 5:16

And, ye fathers, provoke not your children to wrath: but bring them up in the nurture and admonition of the Lord.

Seems Uncaring Toward Your Children

WHEN YOUR HUSBAND . . .

The Lord your God which goeth before you, he shall fight
for you, according to all that he did for you in Egypt
before your eyes.
DEUTERONOMY 1:30

For the eyes of the Lord run to and fro throughout the
whole earth, to shew himself strong in the behalf of
them whose heart is perfect toward him.
2 CHRONICLES 16:9A

But thou, O Lord, art a shield for me; my glory, and the
lifter up of mine head.
PSALM 3:3

The Lord is nigh unto them that are of a broken heart;
and saveth such as be of a contrite spirit.
PSALM 34:18

Yet the Lord will command his lovingkindness in the daytime, and in the night his song shall be with me, and my prayer unto the God of my life.
PSALM 42:8

The Lord will perfect that which concerneth me: thy mercy, O Lord, endureth for ever: forsake not the works of thine own hands.
PSALM 138:8

But I say unto you, Love your enemies, bless them that curse you, do good to them that hate you, and pray for them which despitefully use you, and persecute you.
MATTHEW 5:44

And now abideth faith, hope, charity, these three; but the greatest of these is charity.
1 CORINTHIANS 13:13

And walk in love, as Christ also hath loved us, and hath given himself for us an offering and a sacrifice to God for a sweet-smelling savour.
EPHESIANS 5:2

Forbearing one another, and forgiving one another, if any man have a quarrel against any: even as Christ forgave you, so also do ye.
COLOSSIANS 3:13

Must Be Away from Home

WHEN YOUR HUSBAND . . .

A man that hath friends must shew himself friendly: and there is a friend that sticketh closer than a brother.
PROVERBS 18:24

Make no friendship with an angry man; and with a furious man thou shalt not go.
PROVERBS 22:24

Faithful are the wounds of a friend; but the kisses of an enemy are deceitful.
Ointment and perfume rejoice the heart: so doth the sweetness of a man's friend by hearty counsel.
Thine own friend, and thy father's friend, forsake not; neither go into thy brother's house in the day of thy calamity: for better is a neighbour that is near than a brother far off.
PROVERBS 27:6,9-10

A friend loveth at all times, and a brother is born for adversity.
PROVERBS 17:17

Two are better than one; because they have a good reward for their labour. For if they fall, the one will lift up his fellow: but woe to him that is alone when he falleth; for he hath not another to help him up.
ECCLESIASTES 4:9-10

For the mountains shall depart, and the hills be removed; but my kindness shall not depart from thee, neither shall the covenant of my peace be removed, saith the Lord that hath mercy on thee.
ISAIAH 54:10

For whosoever shall do the will of my Father which is in heaven, the same is my brother, and sister, and mother.
MATTHEW 12:50

But when thou art bidden, go and sit down in the lowest room; that when he that bade thee cometh, he may say unto thee, Friend, go up higher: then shalt thou have worship in the presence of them that sit at meat with thee.
LUKE 14:10

I will not leave you comfortless: I will come to you.
JOHN 14:18

This is my commandment, That ye love one another, as
I have loved you.
Greater love hath no man than this, that a man lay down
his life for his friends.
Ye are my friends, if ye do whatsoever I command you.
Henceforth I call you not servants; for the servant knoweth
not what his lord doeth: but I have called you friends; for
all things that I have heard of my Father I have made
known unto you.
Ye have not chosen me, but I have chosen you, and ordained
you, that ye should go and bring forth fruit, and that your
fruit should remain: that whatsoever ye shall ask of the
Father in my name, he may give it you.
JOHN 15:12-16

Or he that exhorteth, on exhortation: he that giveth, let
him do it with simplicity; he that ruleth, with diligence;
he that sheweth mercy, with cheerfulness.
ROMANS 12:8

But if any provide not for his own, and specially for those
of his own house, he hath denied the faith, and is worse
than an infidel.
1 TIMOTHY 5:8

I am a companion of all them that fear thee, and of them that keep thy precepts.

PSALM 119:63

Becomes Distant or Quiet

For in thee, O Lord, do I hope: thou wilt hear, O Lord my God.
PSALM 38:15

Why art thou cast down, O my soul? and why art thou disquieted within me? hope in God: for shall yet praise him, who is the health of my countenance, and my God.
PSALM 43:5

But I will hope continually, and will yet praise thee more and more.
PSALM 71:14

I am a companion of all them that fear thee, and of them that keep thy precepts.
PSALM 119:63

Happy is he that hath the God of Jacob for his help, whose
hope is in the Lord his God.
PSALM 146:5

Let not thine heart envy sinners: but be thou in the fear
of the Lord all the day long.
For surely there is an end; and thine expectation shall not
be cut off.
PROVERBS 23:17-18

Blessed are the merciful: for they shall obtain mercy.
But I say unto you, That ye resist not evil: but whosoever
shall smite thee on thy right cheek, turn to him the other
also.
But I say unto you, Love your enemies, bless them that
curse you, do good to them that hate you, and pray for
them which despitefully use you, and persecute you.
MATTHEW 5:7,39,44

And forgive us our debts, as we forgive our debtors.
For if ye forgive men their trespasses, your heavenly
Father will also forgive you:
But if ye forgive not men their trespasses, neither will
your Father forgive your trespasses.
MATTHEW 6:12,14-15

Then came Peter to him, and said, Lord, how oft shall my
brother sin against me, and I forgive him? till seven times?
Jesus saith unto him, I say not unto thee, Until seven
times: but, Until seventy times seven.
MATTHEW 18:21-22

Hope deferred maketh the heart sick: but when the desire
cometh, it is a tree of life.
PROVERBS 13:12

Now the God of hope fill you with all joy and peace in
believing, that ye may abound in hope, through the power
of the Holy Ghost.
ROMANS 15:13

And God is able to make all grace abound toward you;
that ye, always having all sufficiency in all things, may
abound to every good work.
2 CORINTHIANS 9:8

Therefore I take pleasure in infirmities, in reproaches, in
necessities, in persecutions, in distresses for Christ's sake:
for when I am weak, then am I strong.
2 CORINTHIANS 12:10

Put on the whole armour of God, that ye may be able to
stand against the wiles of the devil.
Wherefore take unto you the whole armour of God, that
ye may be able to withstand in the evil day, and having
done all, to stand.
Praying always with all prayer and supplication in the
Spirit, and watching thereunto with all perseverance and
supplication for all saints.
EPHESIANS 6:11,13,18

That he would grant you, according to the riches of his glory, to be strengthened with might by his Spirit in the inner man.

Becomes Abusive Toward You or the Children

WHEN YOUR HUSBAND . . .

For I will be merciful to their unrighteousness, and their
sins and their iniquities will I remember no more.
HEBREWS 8:12

Who can understand his errors? cleanse thou me from
secret faults.
PSALM 19:12

And forgive us our debts, as we forgive our debtors.
MATTHEW 6:12

Remember not the sins of my youth, nor my transgressions: according to thy mercy remember thou me for thy
goodness' sake, O Lord.
For thy name's sake, O Lord, pardon mine iniquity; for it
is great.
Look upon mine affliction and my pain; and forgive all
my sins.
PSALM 25:7,11,18

I acknowledged my sin unto thee, and mine iniquity have
I not hid. I said, I will confess my transgressions unto the
Lord; and thou forgavest the iniquity of my sin.
PSALM 32:5

Create in me a clean heart, O God; and renew a right spirit
within me.
PSALM 51:10

Cast thy burden upon the Lord, and he shall sustain thee:
he shall never suffer the righteous to be moved.
PSALM 55:22

Help us, O God of our salvation, for the glory of thy
name: and deliver us, and purge away our sins, for thy
name's sake.
PSALM 79:9

As far as the east is from the west, so far hath he removed
our transgressions from us.
PSALM 103:12

Great peace have they which love thy law: and nothing
shall offend them.
PSALM 119:165

Lo, children are an heritage of the Lord: and the fruit of
the womb is his reward.
PSALM 127:3

But there is forgiveness with thee, that thou mayest be feared.
PSALM 130:4

Be careful for nothing; but in every thing by prayer and
supplication with thanksgiving let your requests be made
known unto God.
PHILIPPIANS 4:6

Behold, I give unto you power to tread on serpents and
scorpions, and over all the power of the enemy: and nothing shall by any means hurt you.
LUKE 10:19

Fear thou not; for I am with thee: be not dismayed; for I am thy God: I will strengthen thee; yea, I will help thee; yea, I will uphold thee with the right hand of my righteousness.
ISAIAH 41:10

For the Lord God will help me; therefore shall I not be confounded: therefore have I set my face like a flint, and I know that I shall not be ashamed.
ISAIAH 50:7

Seek ye the Lord while he may be found, call ye upon him while he is near: Let the wicked forsake his way, and the unrighteous man his thoughts: and let him return unto the Lord, and he will have mercy upon him; and to our God, for he will abundantly pardon.
ISAIAH 55:6-7

It were better for him that a millstone were hanged about his neck, and he cast into the sea, than that he should offend one of these little ones.
LUKE 17:2

And shall not God avenge his own elect, which cry day and night unto him, though he bear long with them? I tell you that he will avenge them speedily.
LUKE 18:7-8A

But if we walk in the light, as he is in the light, we have fellowship one with another, and the blood of Jesus Christ his Son cleanseth us from all sin.
If we confess our sins, he is faithful and just to forgive us our sins, and to cleanse us from all unrighteousness.
1 JOHN 1:7,9

He healeth the broken in heart, and bindeth up their wounds.

PSALM 147:3

Blessed be God, even the Father of our Lord Jesus Christ, the Father of mercies, and the God of all comfort; Who comforteth us in all our tribulation, that we may be able to comfort them which are in any trouble, by the comfort wherewith we ourselves are comforted of God.

2 CORINTHIANS 1:3-4

My little children, these things write I unto you, that ye sin not. And if any man sin, we have an advocate with the Father, Jesus Christ the righteous: And he is the propitiation for our sins: and not for ours only, but also for the sins of the whole world.

1 JOHN 2:1-2

Seems Jealous of Your Attention Toward the Children

WHEN YOUR HUSBAND . . .

Behold, thou desirest truth in the inward parts: and in
the hidden part thou shalt make me to know wisdom.
Create in me a clean heart, O God; and renew a right spirit
within me.
PSALM 51:6,10

In God I will praise his word, in God I have put my trust;
I will not fear what flesh can do unto me.
PSALM 56:4

Teach me thy way, O Lord; I will walk in thy truth: unite
my heart to fear thy name.
PSALM 86:11

Trust in the Lord with all thine heart; and lean not unto
thine own understanding. In all thy ways acknowledge
him, and he shall direct thy paths.
For the Lord shall be thy confidence.
PROVERBS 3:5-6,26A

Finally, my brethren, be strong in the Lord, and in the
power of his might.
EPHESIANS 6:10

The fear of man bringeth a snare: but whoso putteth his trust in the Lord shall be safe.
PROVERBS 29:25

Set me as a seal upon thine heart, as a seal upon thine arm: for love is strong as death; jealousy is cruel as the grave: the coals thereof are coals of fire, which hath a most vehement flame.
SONG OF SOLOMON 8:6

Behold, God is my salvation; I will trust, and not be afraid: for the Lord Jehovah is my strength and my song; he also is become my salvation.
ISAIAH 12:2

Charity suffereth long, and is kind; charity envieth not; charity vaunteth not itself, is not puffed up,
Doth not behave itself unseemly, seeketh not her own, is not easily provoked, thinketh no evil.
1 CORINTHIANS 13:4-5

For the weapons of our warfare are not carnal, but mighty through God to the pulling down of strong holds.
2 CORINTHIANS 10:4

If any of you lack wisdom, let him ask of God, that giveth to all men liberally, and upbraideth not; and it shall be given him.
JAMES 1:5

Beloved, think it not strange concerning the fiery trial which is to try you, as though some strange thing happened unto you.
1 PETER 4:12

Your Work

WHEN YOU MUST BALANCE
FAMILY AND CAREER

One that ruleth well his own house, having his children
in subjection with all gravity;
For if a man know not how to rule his own house, how
shall he take care of the church of God?
1 TIMOTHY 3:4-5

But if any provide not for his own, and specially for those
of his own house, he hath denied the faith, and is worse
than an infidel.
1 TIMOTHY 5:8

Only take heed to thyself, and keep thy soul diligently,
lest thou forget the things which thine eyes have seen,
and lest they depart from thy heart all the days of thy
life: but teach them thy sons, and thy sons' sons.
DEUTERONOMY 4:9

Moreover I will establish his kingdom for ever, if he be
constant to do my commandments and my judgments, as
at this day.
1 CHRONICLES 28:7

For he established a testimony in Jacob, and appointed a
law in Israel, which he commanded our fathers, that they
should make them known to their children:
That the generation to come might know them, even the
children which should be born; who should arise and
declare them to their children:
That they might set their hope in God, and not forget the
works of God, but keep his commandments.
PSALM 78:5-7

And, ye fathers, provoke not your children to wrath: but
bring them up in the nurture and admonition of the Lord.
EPHESIANS 6:4

So teach us to number our days, that we may apply our
hearts unto wisdom.
PSALM 90:12

Blessed is every one that feareth the Lord; that walketh
in his ways. For thou shalt eat the labour of thine hands:
happy shalt thou be, and it shall be well with thee. Thy
wife shall be as a fruitful vine by the sides of thine house:
thy children like olive plants round about thy table. Behold, that thus shall the man be blessed that feareth the
Lord.
PSALM 128:1-4

The soul of the sluggard desireth, and hath nothing: but
the soul of the diligent shall be made fat.
PROVERBS 13:4

The just man walketh in his integrity: his children are
blessed after him.
PROVERBS 20:7

Train up a child in the way he should go: and when he is
old, he will not depart from it.
PROVERBS 22:6

Through wisdom is an house builded; and by understanding it is established.
PROVERBS 24:3

Walk in wisdom toward them that are without, redeeming
the time.
COLOSSIANS 4:5

But seek ye first the kingdom of God, and his righteousness; and all these things shall be added unto you.

MATTHEW 6:33

Correct thy son, and he shall give thee rest; yea, he shall give delight unto thy soul.
PROVERBS 29:17

And all thy children shall be taught of the Lord; and great shall be the peace of thy children.
In righteousness shalt thou be established: thou shalt be far from oppression; for thou shalt not fear: and from terror; for it shall not come near thee.
ISAIAH 54:13-14

See then that ye walk circumspectly, not as fools, but as wise, Redeeming the time, because the days are evil.
EPHESIANS 5:15-16

A man's heart deviseth his way: but the Lord directeth his steps.
PROVERBS 16:9

Who can find a virtuous woman? for her price is far above rubies.

The heart of her husband doth safely trust in her, so that he shall have no need of spoil.

She will do him good and not evil all the days of her life.

She seeketh wool, and flax, and worketh willingly with her hands.

She is like the merchants' ships; she bringeth her food from afar.

She riseth also while it is yet night, and giveth meat to her household, and a portion to her maidens.

She considereth a field, and buyeth it: with the fruit of her hands she planteth a vineyard.

She girdeth her loins with strength, and strengtheneth her arms.

She perceiveth that her merchandise is good: her candle goeth not out by night.

She layeth her hands to the spindle, and her hands hold the distaff.

She stretcheth out her hand to the poor; yea, she reacheth forth her hands to the needy.

She is not afraid of the snow for her household: for all her household are clothed with scarlet.

She maketh herself coverings of tapestry; her clothing is silk and purple.

Her husband is known in the gates, when he sitteth among the elders of the land.

She maketh fine linen, and selleth it; and delivereth girdles unto the merchant.

Strength and honour are her clothing; and she shall rejoice in time to come.

She openeth her mouth with wisdom; and in her tongue is the law of kindness.

She looketh well to the ways of her household, and eateth not the bread of idleness.

Her children arise up, and call her blessed; her husband also, and he praiseth her.

Many daughters have done virtuously, but thou excellest them all.

Favour is deceitful, and beauty is vain: but a woman that feareth the Lord, she shall be praised. Give her of the fruit of her hands; and let her own works praise her in the gates.

PROVERBS 31:10-30

And wisdom and knowledge shall be the stability of thy times, and strength of salvation: the fear of the Lord is his treasure.

When Your Daily Duties Become a Drudgery

YOUR WORK

I will instruct thee and teach thee in the way which thou
shalt go: I will guide thee with mine eye.
PSALM 32:8

For in thee, O Lord, do I hope: thou wilt hear, O Lord my
God.
PSALM 38:15

Why art thou cast down, O my soul? and why art thou
disquieted within me? hope in God: for shall yet praise
him, who is the health of my countenance, and my God.
PSALM 43:5

Happy is he that hath the God of Jacob for his help, whose
hope is in the Lord his God.
PSALM 146:5

Hope deferred maketh the heart sick: but when the desire
cometh, it is a tree of life.
PROVERBS 13:12

Let not thine heart envy sinners: but be thou in the fear
of the Lord all the day long.
For surely there is an end; and thine expectation shall not
be cut off.
PROVERBS 23:17-18

The glory of this latter house shall be greater than of
the former, saith the Lord of hosts: and in this place will
I give peace, saith the Lord of hosts.
HAGGAI 2:9

Now the God of hope fill you with all joy and peace in
believing, that ye may abound in hope, through the power
of the Holy Ghost.
ROMANS 15:13

For which cause we faint not; but though our outward
man perish, yet the inward man is renewed day by day.
2 CORINTHIANS 4:16

And God is able to make all grace abound toward you;
that ye, always having all sufficiency in all things, may
abound to every good work.
2 CORINTHIANS 9:8

Therefore I take pleasure in infirmities, in reproaches, in
necessities, in persecutions, in distresses for Christ's sake:
for when I am weak, then am I strong.
2 CORINTHIANS 12:10

But I will hope continually, and will yet praise thee more
and more.
PSALM 71:14

That he would grant you, according to the riches of his
glory, to be strengthened with might by his Spirit in the
inner man.
EPHESIANS 3:16

Put on the whole armour of God, that ye may be able to
stand against the wiles of the devil.
Wherefore take unto you the whole armour of God, that
ye may be able to withstand in the evil day, and having
done all, to stand.
Praying always with all prayer and supplication in the
Spirit, and watching thereunto with all perseverance and
supplication for all saints.
EPHESIANS 6:11,13,18

And the peace of God, which passeth all understanding,
shall keep your hearts and minds through Christ Jesus.
PHILIPPIANS 4:7

Wherefore gird up the loins of your mind, be sober, and
hope to the end for the grace that is to be brought unto
you at the revelation of Jesus Christ;
But the word of the Lord endureth for ever. And this is
the word which by the gospel is preached unto you.
1 PETER 1:13,25

And let us not be weary in well doing: for in due season we shall reap, if we faint not.

GALATIANS 6:9

When No One Seems to Appreciate Your Efforts

YOUR WORK

Many are the afflictions of the righteous: but the Lord
delivereth him out of them all.
PSALM 34:19

This thou hast seen, O Lord: keep not silence: O Lord, be
not far from me.
PSALM 35:22

Cast thy burden upon the Lord, and he shall sustain thee:
he shall never suffer the righteous to be moved.
PSALM 55:22

He only is my rock and my salvation; he is my defence; I
shall not be greatly moved.
PSALM 62:2

The Lord will perfect that which concerneth me: thy
mercy, O Lord, endureth for ever: forsake not the works
of thine own hands.
PSALM 138:8

Trust in the Lord with all thine heart; and lean not unto thine own understanding. In all thy ways acknowledge him, and he shall direct thy paths.
PROVERBS 3:5-6

He that handleth a matter wisely shall find good: and whoso trusteth in the Lord, happy is he.
PROVERBS 16:20

Whoso putteth his trust in the Lord shall be safe.
PROVERBS 29:25B

Whatsoever thy hand findeth to do, do it with thy might; for there is no work, nor device, nor knowledge, nor wisdom, in the grave, whither thou goest.
ECCLESIASTES 9:10

For the Lord Jehovah is my strength and my song; he also is become my salvation.
ISAIAH 12:2B

Trust ye in the Lord for ever: for in the Lord Jehovah is everlasting strength.
ISAIAH 26:4

What shall we then say to these things? If God be for us, who can be against us?
ROMANS 8:31

O Lord, be gracious unto us; we have waited for thee: be thou their arm every morning, our salvation also in the time of trouble.
ISAIAH 33:2

Fear thou not; for I am with thee: be not dismayed; for I am thy God: I will strengthen thee; yea, I will help thee; yea, I will uphold thee with the right hand of my right-eousness.
ISAIAH 41:10

Therefore I will look unto the Lord; I will wait for the God of my salvation: my God will hear me.
MICAH 7:7

Be ye angry, and sin not: let not the sun go down upon your wrath:
Let all bitterness, and wrath, and anger, and clamour, and evil speaking, be put away from you, with all malice.
EPHESIANS 4:26,31

Looking diligently lest any man fail of the grace of God; lest any root of bitterness springing up trouble you, and thereby many be defiled.
HEBREWS 12:15

Beloved, think it not strange concerning the fiery trial which is to try you, as though some strange thing happened unto you: But rejoice, inasmuch as ye are partakers of Christ's sufferings; that, when his glory shall be revealed, ye may be glad also with exceeding joy.
1 PETER 4:12-13

That thine alms may be in secret: and thy Father which seeth in secret himself shall reward thee openly.

MATTHEW 6:4

When You are Your Family's Sole Support

YOUR WORK

The Lord is good, a strong hold in the day of trouble;
and he knoweth them that trust in him.
NAHUM 1:7

For thou art my rock and my fortress; therefore for thy
name's sake lead me, and guide me.
PSALM 31:3

I will instruct thee and teach thee in the way which thou
shalt go: I will guide thee with mine eye.
PSALM 32:8

Thou shalt guide me with thy counsel, and afterward
receive me to glory.
PSALM 73:24

For the Lord giveth wisdom: out of his mouth cometh
knowledge and understanding.
PROVERBS 2:6

Trust in the Lord with all thine heart; and lean not unto
thine own understanding.
PROVERBS 3:5

He becometh poor that dealeth with a slack hand: but the
hand of the diligent maketh rich.
PROVERBS 10:4

The hand of the diligent shall bear rule: but the slothful
shall be under tribute.
PROVERBS 12:24

The soul of the sluggard desireth, and hath nothing: but
the soul of the diligent shall be made fat.
PROVERBS 13:4

Without counsel purposes are disappointed: but in the
multitude of counsellors they are established.
PROVERBS 15:22

Love not sleep, lest thou come to poverty; open thine eyes,
and thou shalt be satisfied with bread.
PROVERBS 20:13

Seest thou a man diligent in his business? he shall stand
before kings; he shall not stand before mean men.
PROVERBS 22:29

Through wisdom is an house builded; and by understanding it is established.
PROVERBS 24:3

Who can find a virtuous woman? for her price is far above
rubies.
Strength and honour are her clothing; and she shall rejoice
in time to come.
She openeth her mouth with wisdom; and in her tongue
is the law of kindness.
She looketh well to the ways of her household, and eateth
not the bread of idleness.
Her children arise up, and call her blessed; her husband
also, and he praiseth her.
Many daughters have done virtuously, but thou excellest
them all.
Favour is deceitful, and beauty is vain: but a woman that
feareth the Lord, she shall be praised.
Give her of the fruit of her hands; and let her own works
praise her in the gates.
PROVERBS 31:10,25-31

In the morning sow thy seed, and in the evening withhold
not thine hand: for thou knowest not whether shall prosper, either this or that, or whether they both shall be alike
good.
ECCLESIASTES 11:6

Fear thou not; for I am with thee: be not dismayed; for I
am thy God: I will strengthen thee; yea, I will help thee;
yea, I will uphold thee with the right hand of my righteousness.
ISAIAH 41:10

But my God shall supply all your need according to his riches in glory by Christ Jesus.

PHILIPPIANS 4:19

Thus saith the Lord, thy Redeemer, the Holy One of Israel; I am the Lord thy God which teacheth thee to profit, which leadeth thee by the way that thou shouldest go.
ISAIAH 48:17

But seek ye first the kingdom of God, and his righteousness; and all these things shall be added unto you.
MATTHEW 6:33

Not slothful in business; fervent in spirit; serving the Lord.
ROMANS 12:11

When You Feel Guilty about Working Outside the Home

YOUR WORK

The name of the Lord is a strong tower: the righteous
runneth into it, and is safe.
PROVERBS 18:10

Who can find a virtuous woman? for her price is far above
rubies.
Strength and honour are her clothing; and she shall rejoice
in time to come.
She openeth her mouth with wisdom; and in her tongue
is the law of kindness.
She looketh well to the ways of her household, and eateth
not the bread of idleness.
Her children arise up, and call her blessed; her husband
also, and he praiseth her.
Many daughters have done virtuously, but thou excellest
them all.
PROVERBS 31:10,25-29

Commit thy works unto the Lord, and thy thoughts shall
be established.
PROVERBS 16:3

Whatsoever thy hand findeth to do, do it with thy might.
ECCLESIASTES 9:10A

Moreover it is required in stewards, that a man be found
faithful.
1 CORINTHIANS 4:2

For this cause we also, since the day we heard it, do not
cease to pray for you, and to desire that ye might be filled
with the knowledge of his will in all wisdom and spiritual
understanding;
That ye might walk worthy of the Lord unto all pleasing,
being fruitful in every good work, and increasing in the
knowledge of God;
Strengthened with all might, according to his glorious
power, unto all patience and long-suffering with joyfulness.
COLOSSIANS 1:9-11

And whatsoever ye do, do it heartily, as to the Lord, and
not unto men; Knowing that of the Lord ye shall receive
the reward of the inheritance: for ye serve the Lord
Christ.
COLOSSIANS 3:22-23

When You are Fearful for Your Child's Safety

YOUR WORK

The Lord is my light and my salvation; whom shall I fear?
the Lord is the strength of my life; of whom shall I be
afraid?
Though an host should encamp against me, my heart shall
not fear: though war should rise against me, in this will
I be confident.
PSALM 27:1,3

He that dwelleth in the secret place of the most High
shall abide under the shadow of the Almighty.
He shall cover thee with his feathers, and under his wings
shalt thou trust: his truth shall be thy shield and buckler.
Thou shalt not be afraid for the terror by night; nor for
the arrow that flieth by day; Nor for the pestilence that
walketh in darkness; nor for the destruction that wasteth
at noonday. A thousand shall fall at thy side, and ten
thousand at thy right hand; but it shall not come nigh
thee.
PSALM 91:1,4-7

There shall no evil befall thee, neither shall any plague
come nigh thy dwelling.
For he shall give his angels charge over thee, to keep thee
in all thy ways.
PSALM 91:10-11

Great peace have they which love thy law: and nothing
shall offend them.
PSALM 119:165

Be not afraid of sudden fear, neither of the desolation of
the wicked, when it cometh.
For the Lord shall be thy confidence, and shall keep thy
foot from being taken.
PROVERBS 3:25-26

A time to be born, and a time to die; a time to plant, and
a time to pluck up that which is planted.
ECCLESIASTES 3:2

Fear thou not; for I am with thee: be not dismayed; for I
am thy God: I will strengthen thee; yea, I will help thee;
yea, I will uphold thee with the right hand of my righteousness.
ISAIAH 41:10

In righteousness shalt thou be established: thou shalt be
far from oppression; for thou shalt not fear: and from
terror; for it shall not come near thee.
ISAIAH 54:14

Peace I leave with you, my peace I give unto you: not as the world giveth, give I unto you. Let not your heart be troubled, neither let it be afraid.
JOHN 14:27

For ye have not received the spirit of bondage again to fear; but ye have received the Spirit of adoption, whereby we cry, Abba, Father.
ROMANS 8:15

Be careful for nothing; but in every thing by prayer and supplication with thanksgiving let your requests be made known unto God.
And the peace of God, which passeth all understanding, shall keep your hearts and minds through Christ Jesus.
Finally, brethren, whatsoever things are true, whatsoever things are honest, whatsoever things are just, whatsoever things are pure, whatsoever things are lovely, whatsoever things are of good report; if there be any virtue, and if there be any praise, think on these things.
PHILIPPIANS 4:6-8

For God hath not given us the spirit of fear; but of power, and of love, and of a sound mind.
2 TIMOTHY 1:7

There is no fear in love; but perfect love casteth out fear: because fear hath torment. He that feareth is not made perfect in love.
1 JOHN 4:18

Thou wilt keep him in perfect peace, whose mind is stayed on thee: because he trusteth in thee.

ISAIAH 26:3

Your Daily Schedule

WHEN YOU FEEL DISORGANIZED

Shew me thy ways, O Lord; teach me thy paths.
PSALM 25:4

I will instruct thee and teach thee in the way which thou
shalt go: I will guide thee with mine eye.
PSALM 32:8

Cast thy burden upon the Lord, and he shall sustain thee:
he shall never suffer the righteous to be moved.
PSALM 55:22

Trust in the Lord with all thine heart; and lean not unto
thine own understanding. In all thy ways acknowledge
him, and he shall direct thy paths.
PROVERBS 3:5-6

A man's heart deviseth his way: but the Lord directeth
his steps.
PROVERBS 16:9

And thine ears shall hear a word behind thee, saying, This
is the way, walk ye in it, when ye turn to the right hand,
and when ye turn to the left.
ISAIAH 30:21

He giveth power to the faint; and to them that have no
might he increaseth strength.
ISAIAH 40:29

When thou passest through the waters, I will be with
thee; and through the rivers, they shall not overflow thee:
when thou walkest through the fire, thou shalt not be
burned; neither shall the flame kindle upon thee.
ISAIAH 43:2

For God is not the author of confusion, but of peace, as
in all churches of the saints.
1 CORINTHIANS 14:33

Be careful for nothing; but in every thing by prayer and
supplication with thanksgiving let your requests be made
known unto God.
And the peace of God, which passeth all understanding,
shall keep your hearts and minds through Christ Jesus.
PHILIPPIANS 4:6-7

If any of you lack wisdom, let him ask of God, that giveth
to all men liberally, and upbraideth not; and it shall be
given him.
JAMES 1:5

For the Lord God will help me; therefore shall I not be confounded.

ISAIAH 50:7A

When You Feel Overwhelmed by Your Responsibilities

YOUR DAILY SCHEDULE

The name of the Lord is a strong tower: the righteous runneth into it, and is safe.
PROVERBS 18:10

That we henceforth be no more children, tossed to and fro, and carried about with every wind of doctrine, by the sleight of men, and cunning craftiness, whereby they lie in wait to deceive; But speaking the truth in love, may grow up into him in all things, which is the head, even Christ.
EPHESIANS 4:14-15

Let us hear the conclusion of the whole matter: Fear God, and keep his commandments: for this is the whole duty of man.
ECCLESIASTES 12:13

Moreover it is required in stewards, that a man be found faithful.
1 CORINTHIANS 4:2

But we all, with open face beholding as in a glass the glory of the Lord, are changed into the same image from glory to glory, even as by the Spirit of the Lord.
2 CORINTHIANS 3:18

For though we walk in the flesh, we do not war after the flesh: For the weapons of our warfare are not carnal, but mighty through God to the pulling down of strong holds; Casting down imaginations, and every high thing that exalteth itself against the knowledge of God, and bringing into captivity every thought to the obedience of Christ.

2 CORINTHIANS 10:3-5

Whatsoever thy hand findeth to do, do it with thy might.

ECCLESIASTES 9:10A

Being confident of this very thing, that he which hath begun a good work in you will perform it until the day of Jesus Christ:
And this I pray, that your love may abound yet more and more in knowledge and in all judgment; That ye may approve things that are excellent; that ye may be sincere and without offence till the day of Christ.

PHILIPPIANS 1:6,9-10

For this cause we also, since the day we heard it, do not cease to pray for you, and to desire that ye might be filled with the knowledge of his will in all wisdom and spiritual understanding; That ye might walk worthy of the Lord unto all pleasing, being fruitful in every good work, and increasing in the knowledge of God; Strengthened with all might, according to his glorious power, unto all patience and long-suffering with joyfulness.

COLOSSIANS 1:9-11

Let the word of Christ dwell in you richly in all wisdom; teaching and admonishing one another in psalms and hymns and spiritual songs, singing with grace in your hearts to the Lord.

COLOSSIANS 3:16

When You Become Bored

YOUR DAILY SCHEDULE

Be of good courage, and he shall strengthen your heart,
all ye that hope in the Lord.
PSALM 31:24

I will instruct thee and teach thee in the way which thou
shalt go: I will guide thee with mine eye.
PSALM 32:8

For in thee, O Lord, do I hope: thou wilt hear, O Lord my
God.
PSALM 38:15

Why art thou cast down, O my soul? and why art thou
disquieted within me? hope in God: for shall yet praise
him, who is the health of my countenance, and my God.
PSALM 43:5

Happy is he that hath the God of Jacob for his help, whose
hope is in the Lord his God.
PSALM 146:5

Hope deferred maketh the heart sick: but when the desire
cometh, it is a tree of life.
PROVERBS 13:12

Let not thine heart envy sinners: but be thou in the fear
of the Lord all the day long. For surely there is an end;
and thine expectation shall not be cut off.
PROVERBS 23:17-18

Who against hope believed in hope, that he might become
the father of many nations, according to that which was
spoken, So shall thy seed be.
ROMANS 4:18

Now the God of hope fill you with all joy and peace in
believing, that ye may abound in hope, through the power
of the Holy Ghost.
ROMANS 15:13

And God is able to make all grace abound toward you;
that ye, always having all sufficiency in all things, may
abound to every good work.
2 CORINTHIANS 9:8

Therefore I take pleasure in infirmities, in reproaches, in
necessities, in persecutions, in distresses for Christ's sake:
for when I am weak, then am I strong.
2 CORINTHIANS 12:10

That he would grant you, according to the riches of his
glory, to be strengthened with might by his Spirit in the
inner man.
EPHESIANS 3:16

Put on the whole armour of God, that ye may be able to
stand against the wiles of the devil.
Wherefore take unto you the whole armour of God, that
ye may be able to withstand in the evil day, and having
done all, to stand.
Praying always with all prayer and supplication in the
Spirit, and watching thereunto with all perseverance and
supplication for all saints.
EPHESIANS 6:11,13,18

And the peace of God, which passeth all understanding,
shall keep your hearts and minds through Christ Jesus.
PHILIPPIANS 4:7

Wherefore gird up the loins of your mind, be sober, and
hope to the end for the grace that is to be brought unto
you at the revelation of Jesus Christ;
But the word of the Lord endureth for ever. And this is
the word which by the gospel is preached unto you.
1 PETER 1:13,25

But I will hope continually, and will yet praise thee more and more.

PSALM 71:14

When You Continually Procrastinate Tasks

YOUR DAILY SCHEDULE

For I am the Lord, I change not.
MALACHI 3:6A

But thou, O Lord, art a shield for me; my glory, and the lifter
up of mine head.
PSALM 3:3

I will instruct thee and teach thee in the way which thou
shalt go: I will guide thee with mine eye.
PSALM 32:8

Trust in the Lord with all thine heart; and lean not unto
thine own understanding. In all thy ways acknowledge
him, and he shall direct thy paths.
PROVERBS 3:5-6

It is better to trust in the Lord than to put confidence in man.
PSALM 118:8

For the Lord shall be thy confidence, and shall keep thy foot from being taken.
PROVERBS 3:26

A man's heart deviseth his way: but the Lord directeth his steps.
PROVERBS 16:9

He giveth power to the faint; and to them that have no might he increaseth strength.
ISAIAH 40:29

For the Lord God will help me; therefore shall I not be confounded.
ISAIAH 50:7A

Say not ye, There are yet four months, and then cometh harvest? behold, I say unto you, Lift up your eyes, and look on the fields; for they are white already to harvest.
JOHN 4:35

And that, knowing the time, that now it is high time to
awake out of sleep: for now is our salvation nearer than
when we believed.
ROMANS 13:11

Do ye not know that the saints shall judge the world? and
if the world shall be judged by you, are ye unworthy to
judge the smallest matters?
1 CORINTHIANS 6:2

Redeeming the time, because the days are evil.
EPHESIANS 5:16

Walk in wisdom toward them that are without, redeeming
the time.
COLOSSIANS 4:5

If any of you lack wisdom, let him ask of God, that giveth
to all men liberally, and upbraideth not; and it shall be
given him.
JAMES 1:5

Thy word have I hid in mine heart, that I might not sin
against thee.
PSALM 119:11

Commit thy works unto the Lord, and thy thoughts shall be established.

PROVERBS 16:3

When You Feel Robbed of Your Private Time

I have set the Lord always before me: because he is at my
right hand, I shall not be moved.
Therefore my heart is glad, and my glory rejoiceth: my
flesh also shall rest in hope.

PSALM 16:8

Judge me, O Lord; for I have walked in mine integrity: I
have trusted also in the Lord; therefore I shall not slide.
For thy lovingkindness is before mine eyes: and I have
walked in thy truth.

PSALM 26:1,3

Thy testimonies also are my delight and my counsellors.

PSALM 119:24

The wicked flee when no man pursueth: but the righteous
are bold as a lion.
PROVERBS 28:1

I beseech you therefore, brethren, by the mercies of God,
that ye present your bodies a living sacrifice, holy, acceptable unto God, which is your reasonable service.
And be not conformed to this world: but be ye transformed
by the renewing of your mind, that ye may prove what is
that good, and acceptable, and perfect, will of God.
Be kindly affectioned one to another with brotherly love;
in honour preferring one another; Not slothful in business; fervent in spirit; serving the Lord; Rejoicing in hope;
patient in tribulation; continuing instant in prayer; Distributing to the necessity of saints; given to hospitality.
ROMANS 12:1-2,10-13

Watch ye, stand fast in the faith, quit you like men, be
strong.
1 CORINTHIANS 16:13

Casting down imaginations, and every high thing that
exalteth itself against the knowledge of God, and bringing into captivity every thought to the obedience of
Christ.
2 CORINTHIANS 10:5

Wherefore putting away lying, speak every man truth with his neighbour: for we are members one of another.
EPHESIANS 4:25

Finally, my brethren, be strong in the Lord, and in the power of his might.
EPHESIANS 6:10

Be careful for nothing; but in every thing by prayer and supplication with thanksgiving let your requests be made known unto God.
And the peace of God, which passeth all understanding, shall keep your hearts and minds through Christ Jesus.
I can do all things through Christ which strengtheneth me.
PHILIPPIANS 4:6-7,13

Thou therefore, my son, be strong in the grace that is in Christ Jesus.
2 TIMOTHY 2:1

Looking diligently lest any man fail of the grace of God; lest any root of bitterness springing up trouble you, and thereby many be defiled.
HEBREWS 12:15

The steps of a good man are ordered by the Lord: and he delighteth in his way.

PSALM 37:23

When Family Devotions Seem Difficult

Only take heed to thyself, and keep thy soul diligently, lest thou forget the things which thine eyes have seen, and lest they depart from thy heart all the days of thy life: but teach them thy sons, and thy sons' sons.

DEUTERONOMY 4:9

Train up a child in the way he should go: and when he is old, he will not depart from it.

PROVERBS 22:6

Therefore shall ye lay up these my words in your heart and in your soul, and bind them for a sign upon your hand, that they may be as frontlets between your eyes. And ye shall teach them your children, speaking of them when thou sittest in thine house, and when thou walkest by the way, when thou liest down, and when thou risest up.

DEUTERONOMY 11:18-19

That the generation to come might know them, even the
children which should be born; who should arise and
declare them to their children:
That they might set their hope in God, and not forget the
works of God, but keep his commandments.
PSALM 78:6-7

Blessed is every one that feareth the Lord; that walketh
in his ways. For thou shalt eat the labour of thine hands:
happy shalt thou be, and it shall be well with thee. Thy
wife shall be as a fruitful vine by the sides of thine house:
thy children like olive plants round about thy table. Behold, that thus shall the man be blessed that feareth the
Lord.
PSALM 128:1-4

Through wisdom is an house builded; and by understanding it is established.
PROVERBS 24:3

Tell ye your children of it, and let your children tell their
children, and their children another generation.
JOEL 1:3

And these words, which I command thee this day, shall
be in thine heart:
And thou shalt teach them diligently unto thy children,
and shalt talk of them when thou sittest in thine house,
and when thou walkest by the way, and when thou liest
down, and when thou risest up.
DEUTERONOMY 6:6-7

Who can find a virtuous woman? for her price is far above
rubies.
Strength and honour are her clothing; and she shall rejoice
in time to come.
She openeth her mouth with wisdom; and in her tongue
is the law of kindness.
She looketh well to the ways of her household, and eateth
not the bread of idleness.
Her children arise up, and call her blessed; her husband
also, and he praiseth her.
Many daughters have done virtuously, but thou excellest
them all.
Favour is deceitful, and beauty is vain: but a woman that
feareth the Lord, she shall be praised.
Give her of the fruit of her hands; and let her own works
praise her in the gates.
PROVERBS 31:10,25-31

And all thy children shall be taught of the Lord; and great
shall be the peace of thy children.
In righteousness shalt thou be established: thou shalt be
far from oppression; for thou shalt not fear: and from
terror; for it shall not come near thee.
ISAIAH 54:13-14

But seek ye first the kingdom of God, and his righteousness; and all these things shall be added unto you.
MATTHEW 6:33

Correct thy son, and he shall give thee rest; yea, he shall give delight unto thy soul.

PROVERBS 29:17

Your Finances

WHEN IT SEEMS IMPOSSIBLE TO
PAY YOUR BILLS

Be ye strong therefore, and let not your hands be weak:
for your work shall be rewarded.
2 CHRONICLES 15:7

The Lord is good, a strong hold in the day of trouble;
and he knoweth them that trust in him.
NAHUM 1:7

For thou art my rock and my fortress; therefore for thy
name's sake lead me, and guide me.
PSALM 31:3

I will instruct thee and teach thee in the way which thou
shalt go: I will guide thee with mine eye.
PSALM 32:8

Thou shalt guide me with thy counsel, and afterward
receive me to glory.
PSALM 73:24

Though I walk in the midst of trouble, thou wilt revive
me: thou shalt stretch forth thine hand against the wrath
of mine enemies, and thy right hand shall save me.
PSALM 138:7

Love not sleep, lest thou come to poverty; open thine eyes,
and thou shalt be satisfied with bread.
PROVERBS 20:13

Seest thou a man diligent in his business? he shall stand
before kings; he shall not stand before mean men.
PROVERBS 22:29

For the Lord giveth wisdom: out of his mouth cometh
knowledge and understanding.
PROVERBS 2:6

Trust in the Lord with all thine heart; and lean not unto
thine own understanding.
PROVERBS 3:5

He becometh poor that dealeth with a slack hand: but the
hand of the diligent maketh rich.
PROVERBS 10:4

The hand of the diligent shall bear rule: but the slothful
shall be under tribute.
PROVERBS 12:24

The soul of the sluggard desireth, and hath nothing: but
the soul of the diligent shall be made fat.
PROVERBS 13:4

Without counsel purposes are disappointed: but in the
multitude of counsellors they are established.
PROVERBS 15:22

He that hath pity upon the poor lendeth unto the Lord;
and that which he hath given will he pay him again.
PROVERBS 19:17

Through wisdom is an house builded; and by understanding it is established.
PROVERBS 24:3

But seek ye first the kingdom of God, and his righteousness; and all these things shall be added unto you.

MATTHEW 6:33

Not slothful in business; fervent in spirit; serving the Lord.
ROMANS 12:11

He that tilleth his land shall have plenty of bread: but he that followeth after vain persons shall have poverty enough.
PROVERBS 28:19

In the morning sow thy seed, and in the evening withhold not thine hand: for thou knowest not whether shall prosper, either this or that, or whether they both shall be alike good.

ECCLESIASTES 11:6

Fear thou not; for I am with thee: be not dismayed; for I am thy God: I will strengthen thee; yea, I will help thee; yea, I will uphold thee with the right hand of my righteousness.
ISAIAH 41:10

When You Face the Loss of Your Job

YOUR FINANCES

The Lord is good, a strong hold in the day of trouble;
and he knoweth them that trust in him.
NAHUM 1:7

For thou art my rock and my fortress; therefore for thy
name's sake lead me, and guide me.
PSALM 31:3

I will instruct thee and teach thee in the way which thou
shalt go: I will guide thee with mine eye.
PSALM 32:8

Thou shalt guide me with thy counsel, and afterward
receive me to glory.
PSALM 73:24

Trust in the Lord with all thine heart; and lean not unto
thine own understanding.
PROVERBS 3:5

A good man sheweth favour, and lendeth: he will guide
his affairs with discretion.
PSALM 112:5

Though I walk in the midst of trouble, thou wilt revive
me: thou shalt stretch forth thine hand against the wrath
of mine enemies, and thy right hand shall save me.
PSALM 138:7

For the Lord giveth wisdom: out of his mouth cometh
knowledge and understanding.
PROVERBS 2:6

He becometh poor that dealeth with a slack hand: but the
hand of the diligent maketh rich.
PROVERBS 10:4

The hand of the diligent shall bear rule: but the slothful
shall be under tribute.
PROVERBS 12:24

The soul of the sluggard desireth, and hath nothing: but
the soul of the diligent shall be made fat.
PROVERBS 13:4

Not slothful in business; fervent in spirit; serving the
Lord.
ROMANS 12:11

Love not sleep, lest thou come to poverty; open thine eyes, and thou shalt be satisfied with bread.
PROVERBS 20:13

Seest thou a man diligent in his business? he shall stand before kings; he shall not stand before mean men.
PROVERBS 22:29

Through wisdom is an house builded; and by understanding it is established.
PROVERBS 24:3

In the morning sow thy seed, and in the evening withhold not thine hand: for thou knowest not whether shall prosper, either this or that, or whether they both shall be alike good.
ECCLESIASTES 11:6

Therefore I say unto you, Take no thought for your life, what ye shall eat, or what ye shall drink; nor yet for your body, what ye shall put on. Is not the life more than meat, and the body than raiment?
Behold the fowls of the air: for they sow not, neither do they reap, nor gather into barns; yet your heavenly Father feedeth them. Are ye not much better than they?
MATTHEW 6:25-26

But seek ye first the kingdom of God, and his righteousness; and all these things shall be added unto you.
MATTHEW 6:33

Fear thou not; for I am with thee: be not dismayed; for I am thy God: I will strengthen thee; yea, I will help thee; yea, I will uphold thee with the right hand of my righteousness.

ISAIAH 41:10

When Your Husband's Pay Seems Inadequate

YOUR FINANCES

And all these blessings shall come on thee, and overtake thee, if thou shalt hearken unto the voice of the Lord thy God. Blessed shalt thou be in the city, and blessed shalt thou be in the field. Blessed shall be the fruit of thy body, and the fruit of thy ground, and the fruit of thy cattle, the increase of thy kine, and the flocks of thy sheep. Blessed shall be thy basket and thy store. Blessed shalt thou be when thou comest in, and blessed shalt thou be when thou goest out. The Lord shall cause thine enemies that rise up against thee to be smitten before thy face: they shall come out against thee one way, and flee before thee seven ways. The Lord shall command the blessing upon thee in thy storehouses, and in all that thou settest thine hand unto; and he shall bless thee in the land which the Lord thy God giveth thee.
DEUTERONOMY 28:2-8

The Lord is good, a strong hold in the day of trouble; and he knoweth them that trust in him.
NAHUM 1:7

The Lord is my shepherd; I shall not want.
PSALM 23:1

Whatsoever thy hand findeth to do, do it with thy might.
ECCLESIASTES 9:10A

I have been young, and now am old; yet have I not seen the righteous forsaken, nor his seed begging bread.
PSALM 37:25

He becometh poor that dealeth with a slack hand: but the hand of the diligent maketh rich.
PROVERBS 10:4

The hand of the diligent shall bear rule: but the slothful shall be under tribute.
PROVERBS 12:24

Seest thou a man diligent in his business? he shall stand before kings; he shall not stand before mean men.
PROVERBS 22:29

Be thou diligent to know the state of thy flocks, and look well to thy herds.
PROVERBS 27:23

The Lord God hath given me the tongue of the learned, that I should know how to speak a word in season to him that is weary: he wakeneth morning by morning, he wakeneth mine ear to hear as the learned.
ISAIAH 50:4

Therefore, my beloved brethren, be ye stedfast, unmoveable, always abounding in the work of the Lord, forasmuch as ye know that your labour is not in vain in the Lord.
1 CORINTHIANS 15:58

But my God shall supply all your need according to his riches in glory by Christ Jesus.
PHILIPPIANS 4:19

Beloved, I wish above all things that thou mayest prosper and be in health, even as thy soul prospereth.
3 JOHN 2

When Tithing Seems Too Difficult

Vow, and pay unto the Lord your God: let all that be round about him bring presents unto him that ought to be feared.
PSALM 76:11

Honour the Lord with thy substance, and with the firstfruits of all thine increase: So shall thy barns be filled with plenty, and thy presses shall burst out with new wine.
PROVERBS 3:9-10

Cast thy bread upon the waters: for thou shalt find it after many days.
ECCLESIASTES 11:1

Bring ye all the tithes into the storehouse, that there may be meat in mine house, and prove me now herewith, saith the Lord of hosts, if I will not open you the windows of heaven, and pour you out a blessing, that there shall not be room enough to receive it. And I will rebuke the devourer for your sakes, and he shall not destroy the fruits of your ground; neither shall your vine cast her fruit before the time in the field, saith the Lord of hosts.
MALACHI 3:10-11

Upon the first day of the week let every one of you lay by him in store, as God hath prospered him, that there be no gatherings when I come.
1 CORINTHIANS 16:2

. . . Then saith he unto them, Render therefore unto Caesar the things which are Caesar's; and unto God the things that are God's.
MATTHEW 22:21

But this I say, He which soweth sparingly shall reap also sparingly; and he which soweth bountifully shall reap also bountifully. Every man according as he purposeth in his heart, so let him give; not grudgingly, or of necessity: for God loveth a cheerful giver. And God is able to make all grace abound toward you; that ye, always having all sufficiency in all things, may abound to every good work.
2 CORINTHIANS 9:6-8

He that giveth unto the poor shall not lack: but he that
hideth his eyes shall have many a curse.
PROVERBS 28:27

But whoso hath this world's good, and seeth his brother
have need, and shutteth up his bowels of compassion from
him, how dwelleth the love of God in him?
My little children, let us not love in word, neither in
tongue; but in deed and in truth.
1 JOHN 3:17-18

He that hath pity upon the poor lendeth unto the Lord;
and that which he hath given will he pay him again.
PROVERBS 19:17

Give, and it shall be given unto you; good measure, pressed
down, and shaken together, and running over, shall men
give into your bosom. For with the same measure that ye
mete withal it shall be measured to you again.
LUKE 6:38

But my God shall supply all your need according to his riches in glory by Christ Jesus.

When Your Children Need to Learn the Blessing of Work

Be ye strong therefore, and let not your hands be weak: for your work shall be rewarded.
CHRONICLES 15:7

... and who knoweth whether thou art come to the kingdom for such a time as this?
ESTHER 4:14B

He that gathereth in summer is a wise son: but he that sleepeth in harvest is a son that causeth shame.
PROVERBS 10:5

The hand of the diligent shall bear rule: but the slothful shall be under tribute.
PROVERBS 12:24

The soul of the sluggard desireth, and hath nothing: but the soul of the diligent shall be made fat.
PROVERBS 13:4

The thoughts of the diligent tend only to plenteousness; but of every one that is hasty only to want.
PROVERBS 21:5

Seest thou a man diligent in his business? he shall stand before kings; he shall not stand before mean men.
PROVERBS 22:29

The Lord God is my strength, and he will make my feet like hinds' feet, and he will make me to walk upon mine high places.
HABAKKUK 3:19

Say not ye, There are yet four months, and then cometh harvest? behold, I say unto you, Lift up your eyes, and look on the fields; for they are white already to harvest.
JOHN 4:35

As we have therefore opportunity, let us do good unto all men , especially unto them who are of the household of faith.
GALATIANS 6:10

Now unto him that is able to do exceeding abundantly
above all that we ask or think, according to the power
that worketh in us.
EPHESIANS 3:20

I can do all things through Christ which strengtheneth me.
PHILIPPIANS 4:13

If any of you lack wisdom, let him ask of God, that giveth
to all men liberally, and upbraideth not; and it shall be
given him.
JAMES 1:5

Wherefore, beloved, seeing that ye look for such things,
be diligent that ye may be found of him in peace, without
spot, and blameless.
2 PETER 3:14

I know thy works: behold, I have set before thee an open
door, and no man can shut it: for thou hast a little strength,
and hast kept my word, and hast not denied my name.
REVELATION 3:8

I must work the works of him that sent me, while it is
day: the night cometh, when no man can work.
JOHN 9:4

Walk in wisdom toward them that are without, redeeming the time.

COLOSSIANS 4:5

Your Role in the Church

WHEN YOU ARE ASKED TO
TEACH OR ASSUME SPECIAL
ASSIGNMENTS

And thou, Solomon my son, know thou the God of thy
father, and serve him with a perfect heart and with a
willing mind: for the Lord searcheth all hearts, and
understandeth all the imaginations of the thoughts: if
thou seek him, he will be found of thee; but if thou forsake
him, he will cast thee off for ever.

1 CHRONICLES 28:9

I have set the Lord always before me: because he is at my
right hand, I shall not be moved.
Therefore my heart is glad, and my glory rejoiceth: my
flesh also shall rest in hope.

PSALM 16:8-9

For thy lovingkindness is before mine eyes: and I have
walked in thy truth.

PSALM 26:3

The steps of a good man are ordered by the Lord: and
he delighteth in his way.

PSALM 37:23

Make a joyful noise unto the Lord, all ye lands. Serve the
Lord with gladness: come before his presence with singing.
Enter into his gates with thanksgiving, and into his courts
with praise: be thankful unto him, and bless his name.

PSALM 100:1-2,4

Thy testimonies also are my delight and my counsellors.
PSALM 119:24

The wicked flee when no man pursueth: but the righteous
are bold as a lion.
PROVERBS 28:1

I beseech you therefore, brethren, by the mercies of God,
that ye present your bodies a living sacrifice, holy, acceptable unto God, which is your reasonable service.
And be not conformed to this world: but be ye transformed
by the renewing of your mind, that ye may prove what is
that good, and acceptable, and perfect, will of God.
Be kindly affectioned one to another with brotherly love;
in honour preferring one another;
Not slothful in business; fervent in spirit; serving the
Lord; Rejoicing in hope; patient in tribulation; continuing
instant in prayer; Distributing to the necessity of saints;
given to hospitality.
ROMANS 12:1-2,10-13

Watch ye, stand fast in the faith, quit you like men, be
strong.
1 CORINTHIANS 16:13

Finally, my brethren, be strong in the Lord, and in the power of his might.

EPHESIANS 6:10

Casting down imaginations, and every high thing that exalteth itself against the knowledge of God, and bringing into captivity every thought to the obedience of Christ.

2 CORINTHIANS 10:5

Be careful for nothing; but in every thing by prayer and supplication with thanksgiving let your requests be made known unto God.
And the peace of God, which passeth all understanding, shall keep your hearts and minds through Christ Jesus.
I can do all things through Christ which strengtheneth me.

PHILIPPIANS 4:6-7,13

When You Feel Unqualified for Leadership

YOUR ROLE IN THE CHURCH

Be ye strong therefore, and let not your hands be weak:
for your work shall be rewarded.
2 CHRONICLES 15:7

Be of good courage, and he shall strengthen your heart,
all ye that hope in the Lord.
PSALM 31:24

Counsel is mine, and sound wisdom: I am understanding;
I have strength.
PROVERBS 8:14

Fear thou not; for I am with thee: be not dismayed; for I
am thy God: I will strengthen thee; yea, I will help thee;
yea, I will uphold thee with the right hand of my righteousness.
ISAIAH 41:10

The Lord God is my strength, and he will make my feet like hinds' feet, and he will make me to walk upon mine high places.
HABAKKUK 3:19

But ye shall receive power, after that the Holy Ghost is come upon you: and ye shall be witnesses unto me both in Jerusalem, and in all Judaea, and in Samaria, and unto the uttermost part of the earth.
ACTS 1:8

But God hath chosen the foolish things of the world to confound the wise; and God hath chosen the weak things of the world to confound the things which are mighty.
1 CORINTHIANS 1:27

And God is able to make all grace abound toward you; that ye, always having all sufficiency in all things, may abound to every good work.
2 CORINTHIANS 9:8

And he said unto me, My grace is sufficient for thee: for my strength is made perfect in weakness. Most gladly therefore will I rather glory in my infirmities, that the power of Christ may rest upon me.
2 CORINTHIANS 12:9

Now unto him that is able to do exceeding abundantly above all that we ask or think, according to the power that worketh in us.
EPHESIANS 3:20

I can do all things through Christ which strengtheneth me.
PHILIPPIANS 4:13

Cast not away therefore your confidence, which hath great recompense of reward.
For ye have need of patience, that, after ye have done the will of God, ye might receive the promise.
HEBREWS 10:35-36

Through faith also Sara herself received strength to conceive seed, and was delivered of a child when she was past age, because she judged him faithful who had promised.
HEBREWS 11:11

Strengthen ye the weak hands, and confirm the feeble knees.
ISAIAH 35:3

For to one is given by the Spirit the word of wisdom; to another the word of knowledge by the same Spirit.
1 CORINTHIANS 12:8

If any of you lack wisdom, let him ask of God, that giveth to all men liberally, and upbraideth not; and it shall be given him.

JAMES 1:5

When You Hear Slander

Keep me as the apple of the eye, hide me under the shadow
of thy wings.
PSALM 17:8

For in the time of trouble he shall hide me in his pavilion:
in the secret of his tabernacle shall he hide me; he shall
set me up upon a rock.
And now shall mine head be lifted up above mine enemies
round about me: therefore will I offer in his tabernacle
sacrifices of joy; I will sing, yea, I will sing praises unto
the Lord.
PSALM 27:5-6

Thou art my hiding place; thou shalt preserve me from
trouble; thou shalt compass me about with songs of deliverance.
PSALM 32:7

Hide me from the secret counsel of the wicked; from the
insurrection of the workers of iniquity.
PSALM 64:2

Hide not thy face from me in the day when I am in trouble;
incline thine ear unto me: in the day when I call answer
me speedily.
PSALM 102:2

Thy word have I hid in mine heart, that I might not sin
against thee.
Thy word is a lamp unto my feet, and a light unto my
path.
Thou art my hiding place and my shield: I hope in thy
word.
PSALM 119:11,105,114

Hear me speedily, O Lord: my spirit faileth: hide not thy
face from me, lest I be like unto them that go down into
the pit.
Deliver me, O Lord, from mine enemies: I flee unto thee
to hide me. Teach me to do thy will; for thou art my God:
thy spirit is good; lead me into the land of uprightness.
PSALM 143:7,9-10

A word fitly spoken is like apples of gold in pictures of silver.
PROVERBS 25:11

A time to rend, and a time to sew; a time to keep silence, and a time to speak.
ECCLESIASTES 3:7

For by thy words thou shalt be justified, and by thy words thou shalt be condemned.
MATTHEW 12:37

Let no corrupt communication proceed out of your mouth, but that which is good to the use of edifying, that it may minister grace unto the hearers.
EPHESIANS 4:29

Let your speech be alway with grace, seasoned with salt, that ye may know how ye ought to answer every man.
COLOSSIANS 4:6

Wherefore, my beloved brethren, let every man be swift to hear, slow to speak, slow to wrath.
JAMES 1:19

Whoso keepeth his mouth and his tongue keepeth his soul from troubles.

PROVERBS 21:23

But now ye also put off all these; anger, wrath, malice, blasphemy, filthy communication out of your mouth. Lie not one to another, seeing that ye have put off the old man with his deeds . . .
COLOSSIANS 3:8-9

Set a watch, O Lord, before my mouth; keep the door of my lips.
PSALM 141:3

When Someone Has Offended You

Thou shalt not avenge, nor bear any grudge against the children of thy people, but thou shalt love thy neighbour as thyself: I am the Lord.
LEVITICUS 19:18

O Lord my God, in thee do I put my trust: save me from all them that persecute me, and deliver me.
PSALM 7:1

And they that know thy name will put their trust in thee: for thou, Lord, hast not forsaken them that seek thee.
PSALM 9:10

Unto thee, O Lord, do I lift up my soul. O my God, I trust in thee: let me not be ashamed, let not mine enemies triumph over me.
PSALM 25:1-2

Trust in the Lord, and do good; so shalt thou dwell in the land, and verily thou shalt be fed.
Delight thyself also in the Lord; and he shall give thee the desires of thine heart.
Commit thy way unto the Lord; trust also in him; and he shall bring it to pass. And he shall bring forth thy righteousness as the light, and thy judgment as the noonday.
Cease from anger, and forsake wrath: fret not thyself in any wise to do evil.
PSALM 37:3-6,8

Because he hath set his love upon me, therefore will I deliver him: I will set him on high, because he hath known my name. He shall call upon me, and I will answer him: I will be with him in trouble; I will deliver him, and honour him.
PSALM 91:14-15

For the Lord will not cast off his people, neither will he forsake his inheritance.
PSALM 94:14

Say not thou, I will recompense evil; but wait on the Lord, and he shall save thee.
PROVERBS 20:22

For if ye forgive men their trespasses, your heavenly Father will also forgive you.
MATTHEW 6:14

And if he trespass against thee seven times in a day, and seven times in a day turn again to thee, saying, I repent; thou shalt forgive him.
LUKE 17:4

Recompense to no man evil for evil. Provide things honest in the sight of all men.
ROMANS 12:17

Charity suffereth long, and is kind; charity envieth not; charity vaunteth not itself, is not puffed up.
1 CORINTHIANS 13:4

And the servant of the Lord must not strive; but be gentle unto all men, apt to teach, patient.
2 TIMOTHY 2:24

Notwithstanding the Lord stood with me, and strengthened me; that by me the preaching might be fully known, and that all the Gentiles might hear: and I was delivered out of the mouth of the lion. And the Lord shall deliver me from every evil work, and will preserve me unto his heavenly kingdom: to whom be glory for ever and ever. Amen.
2 TIMOTHY 4:17-18

The discretion of a man deferreth his anger; and it is his glory to pass over a transgression.

PROVERBS 19:11

Moreover if thy brother shall trespass against thee, go and tell him his fault between thee and him alone: if he shall hear thee, thou hast gained thy brother. But if he will not hear thee, then take with thee one or two more, that in the mouth of two or three witnesses every word may be established. And if he shall neglect to hear them, tell it unto the church: but if he neglect to hear the church, let him be unto thee as an heathen man and a publican.

MATTHEW 18:15-17

When Church Conflicts Disillusion You

For thou art my rock and my fortress; therefore for thy
name's sake lead me, and guide me.
Pull me out of the net that they have laid privily for me:
for thou art my strength.
Into thine hand I commit my spirit: thou hast redeemed
me, O Lord God of truth.

PSALM 31:3-5

The lip of truth shall be established for ever: but a lying
tongue is but for a moment.

PROVERBS 12:19

Commit thy way unto the Lord; trust also in him; and he
shall bring it to pass.
And he shall bring forth thy righteousness as the light,
and thy judgment as the noonday.
Rest in the Lord, and wait patiently for him: fret not
thyself because of him who prospereth in his way, because
of the man who bringeth wicked devices to pass.

PSALM 37:5-7

For in thee, O Lord, do I hope: thou wilt hear, O Lord my
God.
PSALM 38:15

In my distress I cried unto the Lord, and he heard me.
Deliver my soul, O Lord, from lying lips, and from a
deceitful tongue.
PSALM 120:1-2

Though I walk in the midst of trouble, thou wilt revive
me: thou shalt stretch forth thine hand against the wrath
of mine enemies, and thy right hand shall save me.
PSALM 138:7

Commit thy works unto the Lord, and thy thoughts shall
be established.
PROVERBS 16:3

Say not, I will do so to him as he hath done to me: I will
render to the man according to his work.
PROVERBS 24:29

When thou passest through the waters, I will be with
thee; and through the rivers, they shall not overflow thee:
when thou walkest through the fire, thou shalt not be
burned; neither shall the flame kindle upon thee.
ISAIAH 43:2

And the Lord shall guide thee continually, and satisfy thy soul in drought, and make fat thy bones: and thou shalt be like a watered garden, and like a spring of water, whose waters fail not.
ISAIAH 58:11

I the Lord search the heart, I try the reins, even to give every man according to his ways, and according to the fruit of his doings.
JEREMIAH 17:10

The Lord is good, a strong hold in the day of trouble; and he knoweth them that trust in him.
NAHUM 1:7

And when ye stand praying, forgive, if ye have ought against any: that your Father also which is in heaven may forgive you your trespasses.
But if ye do not forgive, neither will your Father which is in heaven forgive your trespasses.
MARK 11:25-26

And who is he that will harm you, if ye be followers of that which is good?
1 PETER 3:13

Casting all your care upon him; for he careth for you.
1 PETER 5:7

Thou art my hiding place; thou shalt preserve me from trouble; thou shalt compass me about with songs of deliverance.

PSALM 32:7

When A Church Leader Fails

YOUR ROLE IN THE CHURCH

Behold, as the eyes of servants look unto the hand of
their masters, and as the eyes of a maiden unto the hand
of her mistress; so our eyes wait upon the Lord our God,
until that he have mercy upon us.
PSALM 123:2

He that walketh with wise men shall be wise: but a
companion of fools shall be destroyed.
PROVERBS 13:20

Moreover it is required in stewards, that a man be found
faithful.
1 CORINTHIANS 4:2

And whosoever shall give to drink unto one of these little
ones a cup of cold water only in the name of a disciple,
verily I say unto you, he shall in no wise lose his reward.
MATTHEW 10:42

Even as the Son of man came not to be ministered unto,
but to minister, and to give his life a ransom for many.
MATTHEW 20:28

But so shall it not be among you: but whosoever will be
great among you, shall be your minister:
And whosoever of you will be the chiefest, shall be servant
of all.
MARK 10:43-44

And he said, He that shewed mercy on him. Then said
Jesus unto him, Go, and do thou likewise.
LUKE 10:37

And the son said unto him, Father, I have sinned against
heaven, and in thy sight, and am no more worthy to be
called thy son. But the father said to his servants, Bring
forth the best robe, and put it on him; and put a ring on
his hand, and shoes on his feet:
And bring hither the fatted calf, and kill it; and let us eat,
and be merry: For this my son was dead, and is alive again;
he was lost, and is found. And they began to be merry.
LUKE 15:21-24

Verily, verily, I say unto you, The servant is not greater
than his lord; neither he that is sent greater than he that
sent him.
A new commandment I give unto you, That ye love one
another; as I have loved you, that ye also love one another.
JOHN 13:16,34

Now the God of patience and consolation grant you to
be likeminded one toward another according to Christ
Jesus: That ye may with one mind and one mouth glorify
God, even the Father of our Lord Jesus Christ.
Wherefore receive ye one another, as Christ also received
us to the glory of God.
ROMANS 15:5-7

Therefore, my beloved brethren, be ye stedfast, unmoveable, always abounding in the work of the Lord, forasmuch as ye know that your labour is not in vain in the Lord.
1 CORINTHIANS 15:58

Brethren, if a man be overtaken in a fault, ye which are spiritual, restore such an one in the spirit of meekness; considering thyself, lest thou also be tempted. Bear ye one another's burdens, and so fulfil the law of Christ.
As we have therefore opportunity, let us do good unto all men, especially unto them who are of the household of faith.
GALATIANS 6:1-2,10

Be ye therefore followers of God, as dear children; And walk in love, as Christ also hath loved us, and hath given himself for us an offering and a sacrifice to God for a sweet-smelling savour.
EPHESIANS 5:1-2

Forbearing one another, and forgiving one another, if any man have a quarrel against any: even as Christ forgave you, so also do ye.
Servants, obey in all things your masters according to the flesh; not with eye-service, as men-pleasers; but in singleness of heart, fearing God.
COLOSSIANS 3:13,22

Looking unto Jesus the author and finisher of our faith; who for the joy that was set before him endured the cross, despising the shame, and is set down at the right hand of the throne of God.
For consider him that endured such contradiction of sinners against himself, lest ye be wearied and faint in your minds.
HEBREWS 12:2-3

Hereby perceive we the love of God, because he laid down his life for us: and we ought to lay down our lives for the brethren.

1 JOHN 3:16

For even hereunto were ye called: because Christ also suffered for us, leaving us an example, that ye should follow his steps.
1 PETER 2:21

If we confess our sins, he is faithful and just to forgive us our sins, and to cleanse us from all unrighteousness.
1 JOHN 1:9

For all that is in the world, the lust of the flesh, and the lust of the eyes, and the pride of life, is not of the Father, but is of the world.
1 JOHN 2:16

As many as I love, I rebuke and chasten: be zealous therefore, and repent.
REVELATION 3:19

Your Personal Needs

WHEN YOU NEED STRENGTH

For the joy of the Lord is your strength.
NEHEMIAH 8:10B

The Lord is my rock, and my fortress, and my deliverer;
my God, my strength, in whom I will trust; my buckler,
and the horn of my salvation, and my high tower.
PSALM 18:2

Be of good courage, and he shall strengthen your heart,
all ye that hope in the Lord.
PSALM 31:24

Be thou my strong habitation, whereunto I may continually
resort: thou hast given commandment to save me; for
thou art my rock and my fortress.
PSALM 71:3

My soul melteth for heaviness: strengthen thou me
according unto thy word.
PSALM 119:28

A wise man is strong; yea, a man of knowledge increaseth
strength.
PROVERBS 24:5

In the day when I cried thou answeredst me, and strength-
enedst me with strength in my soul.
PSALM 138:3

Fear thou not; for I am with thee: be not dismayed; for I
am thy God: I will strengthen thee; yea, I will help thee;
yea, I will uphold thee with the right hand of my righteousness.
ISAIAH 41:10

The way of the Lord is strength to the upright: but
destruction shall be to the workers of iniquity.
PROVERBS 10:29

Behold, God is my salvation; I will trust, and not be afraid:
for the Lord Jehovah is my strength and my song; he also
is become my salvation.
ISAIAH 12:2

For thus saith the Lord God, the Holy One of Israel; In
returning and rest shall ye be saved; in quietness and in
confidence shall be your strength: and ye would not.
ISAIAH 30:12

He giveth power to the faint; and to them that have no
might he increaseth strength.
But they that wait upon the Lord shall renew their
strength; they shall mount up with wings as eagles; they
shall run, and not be weary; and they shall walk, and not
faint.
ISAIAH 40:29,31

Counsel is mine, and sound wisdom: I am understanding; I have strength.

PROVERBS 8:14

And said, O man greatly beloved, fear not: peace be unto thee, be strong, yea, be strong. And when he had spoken unto me, I was strengthened, and said, Let my lord speak; for thou hast strengthened me.
DANIEL 10:19

Therefore I take pleasure in infirmities, in reproaches, in necessities, in persecutions, in distresses for Christ's sake: for when I am weak, then am I strong.
2 CORINTHIANS 12:10

That he would grant you, according to the riches of his glory, to be strengthened with might by his Spirit in the inner man; That Christ may dwell in your hearts by faith; that ye, being rooted and grounded in love.
EPHESIANS 3:16-17

I can do all things through Christ which strengtheneth me.
PHILIPPIANS 4:13

That ye might walk worthy of the Lord unto all pleasing, being fruitful in every good work, and increasing in the knowledge of God; Strengthened with all might, according to his glorious power, unto all patience and long-suffering with joyfulness; Giving thanks unto the Father, which hath made us meet to be partakers of the inheritance of the saints in light.
COLOSSIANS 1:10-12

The Lord is my light and my salvation; whom shall I fear? the Lord is the strength of my life; of whom shall I be afraid?
Wait on the Lord: be of good courage, and he shall strengthen thine heart: wait, I say, on the Lord.
PSALM 27:1,14

The Lord God is my strength, and he will make my feet like hinds' feet, and he will make me to walk upon mine high places.
HABAKKUK 3:19

In the fear
of the Lord
is strong
confidence: and
his children
shall have a
place of refuge.

PROVERBS 14:26

When You Need to Feel Loved

Delight thyself also in the Lord; and he shall give thee
the desires of thine heart.
Commit thy way unto the Lord; trust also in him; and he
shall bring it to pass.
And he shall bring forth thy righteousness as the light,
and thy judgment as the noonday.
PSALM 37:4-6

And I will betroth thee unto me for ever; yea, I will betroth
thee unto me in righteousness, and in judgment, and in
lovingkindness, and in mercies.
HOSEA 2:19

For God so loved the world, that he gave his only begotten
Son, that whosoever believeth in him should not perish,
but have everlasting life.
JOHN 3:16

He that hath my commandments, and keepeth them, he it is that loveth me: and he that loveth me shall be loved of my Father, and I will love him, and will manifest myself to him.

JOHN 14:21

As the Father hath loved me, so have I loved you: continue ye in my love. If ye keep my commandments, ye shall abide in my love; even as I have kept my Father's commandments, and abide in his love. These things have I spoken unto you, that my joy might remain in you, and that your joy might be full. This is my commandment, That ye love one another, as I have loved you. Greater love hath no man than this, that a man lay down his life for his friends.
These things I command you, that ye love one another.

JOHN 15:9-13,17

For I am persuaded, that neither death, nor life, nor angels, nor principalities, nor powers, nor things present, nor things to come, Nor height, nor depth, nor any other creature, shall be able to separate us from the love of God, which is in Christ Jesus our Lord.

ROMANS 8:38-39

Finally, brethren, whatsoever things are true, whatsoever things are honest, whatsoever things are just, whatsoever things are pure, whatsoever things are lovely, whatsoever things are of good report; if there be any virtue, and if there be any praise, think on these things.

PHILIPPIANS 4:8

And to know the love of Christ, which passeth knowledge,
that ye might be filled with all the fulness of God.
EPHESIANS 3:19

Beloved, let us love one another: for love is of God; and
every one that loveth is born of God, and knoweth God.
He that loveth not knoweth not God; for God is love. In
this was manifested the love of God toward us, because
that God sent his only begotten Son into the world, that
we might live through him. Herein is love, not that we
loved God, but that he loved us, and sent his Son to be
the propitiation for our sins. Beloved, if God so loved us,
we ought also to love one another.
No man hath seen God at any time. If we love one another,
God dwelleth in us, and his love is perfected in us.
And we have known and believed the love that God hath
to us. God is love; and he that dwelleth in love dwelleth
in God, and God in him.
We love him, because he first loved us.
1 JOHN 4:7-12,16,19

For the Father himself loveth you, because ye have loved
me, and have believed that I came out from God.
JOHN 16:27

I love them that love me; and those that seek me early shall find me.

PROVERBS 8:17

When You Need to Forgive

Rejoice not when thine enemy falleth, and let not thine
heart be glad when he stumbleth:
Say not, I will do so to him as he hath done to me: I will
render to the man according to his work.
PROVERBS 24:17,29

If thine enemy be hungry, give him bread to eat; and if
he be thirsty, give him water to drink.
PROVERBS 25:21

Blessed are the merciful: for they shall obtain mercy.
MATTHEW 5:7

But I say unto you, That ye resist not evil: but whosoever
shall smite thee on thy right cheek, turn to him the other
also.
MATTHEW 5:39

The discretion of a man deferreth his anger; and it is his glory to pass over a transgression.
PROVERBS 19:11

But I say unto you, Love your enemies, bless them that curse you, do good to them that hate you, and pray for them which despitefully use you, and persecute you.
MATTHEW 5:44

And forgive us our debts, as we forgive our debtors.
For if ye forgive men their trespasses, your heavenly Father will also forgive you:
But if ye forgive not men their trespasses, neither will your Father forgive your trespasses.
MATTHEW 6:12,14-15

Then came Peter to him, and said, Lord, how oft shall my brother sin against me, and I forgive him? till seven times? Jesus saith unto him, "I say not unto thee, Until seven times: but, Until seventy times seven."
MATTHEW 18:21-22

And when ye stand praying, forgive, if ye have ought against any: that your Father also which is in heaven may forgive you your trespasses.
MARK 11:25

Take heed to yourselves: If thy brother trespass against thee, rebuke him; and if he repent, forgive him.
And if he trespass against thee seven times in a day, and seven times in a day turn again to thee, saying, I repent; thou shalt forgive him.
LUKE 17:3-4

And be ye kind one to another, tenderhearted, forgiving one another, even as God for Christ's sake hath forgiven you.
EPHESIANS 4:32

Pardon, I beseech thee, the iniquity of this people according unto the greatness of thy mercy, and as thou hast forgiven this people, from Egypt even until now.
NUMBERS 14:19

Forbearing one another, and forgiving one another, if any man have a quarrel against any: even as Christ forgave you, so also do ye.
COLOSSIANS 3:13

Not rendering evil for evil, or railing for railing: but contrariwise blessing; knowing that ye are thereunto called, that ye should inherit a blessing.
1 PETER 3:9

Bless them which persecute you: bless, and curse not.
Be not overcome of evil, but overcome evil with good.

When You Need Personal Comfort

And he said, My presence shall go with thee, and I will give thee rest.
EXODUS 33:14

Seek the Lord and his strength, seek his face continually.
1 CHRONICLES 16:11

The righteous also shall hold on his way, and he that hath clean hands shall be stronger and stronger.
JOB 17:9

Yea, though I walk through the valley of the shadow of death, I will fear no evil: for thou art with me; thy rod and thy staff they comfort me.
PSALM 23:4

Be of good courage, and he shall strengthen your heart, all ye that hope in the Lord.
PSALM 31:24

He that dwelleth in the secret place of the most High shall abide under the shadow of the Almighty. I will say of the Lord, He is my refuge and my fortress: my God; in him will I trust. Surely he shall deliver thee from the snare of the fowler, and from the noisome pestilence. He shall cover thee with his feathers, and under his wings shalt thou trust: his truth shall be thy shield and buckler.
PSALM 91:1-4

This is my comfort in my affliction: for thy word hath quickened me.
Thou art my hiding place and my shield: I hope in thy word.
PSALM 119:50,114

Though I walk in the midst of trouble, thou wilt revive me: thou shalt stretch forth thine hand against the wrath of mine enemies, and thy right hand shall save me.
PSALM 138:7

Trust in the Lord with all thine heart; and lean not unto thine own understanding.
PROVERBS 3:5

Fear thou not; for I am with thee: be not dismayed; for I am thy God: I will strengthen thee; yea, I will help thee; yea, I will uphold thee with the right hand of my right-eousness.
For I the Lord thy God will hold thy right hand, saying unto thee, Fear not; I will help thee.
ISAIAH 41:10,13

When thou passest through the waters, I will be with thee; and through the rivers, they shall not overflow thee: when thou walkest through the fire, thou shalt not be burned; neither shall the flame kindle upon thee.
ISAIAH 43:2

For the Lord hath comforted his people, and will have mercy upon his afflicted.
ISAIAH 49:13B

If ye abide in me, and my words abide in you, ye shall ask what ye will, and it shall be done unto you.
JOHN 15:7

Nay, in all these things we are more than conquerors through him that loved us. For I am persuaded, that neither death, nor life, nor angels, nor principalities, nor powers, nor things present, nor things to come, Nor height, nor depth, nor any other creature, shall be able to separate us from the love of God, which is in Christ Jesus our Lord.
ROMANS 8:37-39

Therefore, my beloved brethren, be ye stedfast, unmoveable, always abounding in the work of the Lord, forasmuch as ye know that your labour is not in vain in the Lord.
1 CORINTHIANS 15:58

I will not leave you comfortless: I will come to you.

JOHN 14:18

Watch ye, stand fast in the faith, quit you like men, be strong.
1 CORINTHIANS 16:13

Blessed be God, even the Father of our Lord Jesus Christ, the Father of mercies, and the God of all comfort; Who comforteth us in all our tribulation, that we may be able to comfort them which are in any trouble, by the comfort wherewith we ourselves are comforted of God.
2 CORINTHIANS 1:3-4

Being confident of this very thing, that he which hath begun a good work in you will perform it until the day of Jesus Christ.
PHILIPPIANS 1:6

Therefore, my brethren dearly beloved and longed for, my joy and crown, so stand fast in the Lord, my dearly beloved.
PHILIPPIANS 4:1

Now our Lord Jesus Christ himself, and God, even our Father, which hath loved us, and hath given us everlasting consolation and good hope through grace,
Comfort your hearts, and stablish you in every good word and work.
2 THESSALONIANS 2:16-17

Let us therefore come boldly unto the throne of grace, that we may obtain mercy, and find grace to help in time of need.
HEBREWS 4:16

Looking unto Jesus the author and finisher of our faith; who for the joy that was set before him endured the cross, despising the shame, and is set down at the right hand of the throne of God.
HEBREWS 12:2

Casting all your care upon him; for he careth for you.
1 PETER 5:7

And God shall wipe away all tears from their eyes; and there shall be no more death, neither sorrow, nor crying, neither shall there be any more pain: for the former things are passed away.
REVELATION 21:4

Blessed are they that mourn: for they shall be comforted.

MATTHEW 5:4

When You Need Inner Peace

I will both lay me down in peace, and sleep: for thou, Lord,
only makest me dwell in safety.
PSALM 4:8

But the meek shall inherit the earth; and shall delight
themselves in the abundance of peace.
Mark the perfect man, and behold the upright: for the end
of that man is peace.
PSALM 37:11,37

I will hear what God the Lord will speak: for he will speak
peace unto his people, and to his saints: but let them not
turn again to folly.
PSALM 85:8

Great peace have they which love thy law: and nothing
shall offend them.
PSALM 119:165

Thou wilt keep him in perfect peace, whose mind is stayed
on thee: because he trusteth in thee.
Lord, thou wilt ordain peace for us: for thou also hast
wrought all our works in us.
ISAIAH 26:3,12

For ye shall go out with joy, and be led forth with peace:
the mountains and the hills shall break forth before you
into singing, and all the trees of the field shall clap their
hands.
ISAIAH 55:12

He shall enter into peace: they shall rest in their beds,
each one walking in his uprightness.
ISAIAH 57:2

Peace I leave with you, my peace I give unto you: not as
the world giveth, give I unto you. Let not your heart be
troubled, neither let it be afraid.
JOHN 14:27

These things I have spoken unto you, that in me ye might
have peace. In the world ye shall have tribulation: but be
of good cheer; I have overcome the world.
JOHN 16:33

Therefore being justified by faith, we have peace with God
through our Lord Jesus Christ.
ROMANS 5:1

For to be carnally minded is death; but to be spiritually
minded is life and peace.
ROMANS 8:6

For he that in these things serveth Christ is acceptable
to God, and approved of men.
Let us therefore follow after the things which make for
peace, and things wherewith one may edify another.
ROMANS 14:18-19

Now the God of hope fill you with all joy and peace in
believing, that ye may abound in hope, through the power
of the Holy Ghost.
ROMANS 15:13

Finally, brethren, farewell. Be perfect, be of good comfort,
be of one mind, live in peace; and the God of love and
peace shall be with you.
2 CORINTHIANS 13:11

Grace be to you and peace from God the Father, and from
our Lord Jesus Christ.
GALATIANS 1:3

But the fruit of the Spirit is love, joy, peace, long-suffering,
gentleness, goodness, faith.
GALATIANS 5:22

For he is our peace, who hath made both one, and hath
broken down the middle wall of partition between us.
EPHESIANS 2:14

And let the peace of God rule in your hearts, to the which
also ye are called in one body; and be ye thankful.
COLOSSIANS 3:15

And the fruit of righteousness is sown in peace of them that make peace.

JAMES 3:18

Be careful for nothing; but in every thing by prayer and supplication with thanksgiving let your requests be made known unto God.
And the peace of God, which passeth all understanding, shall keep your hearts and minds through Christ Jesus.
Those things, which ye have both learned, and received, and heard, and seen in me, do: and the God of peace shall be with you.
PHILIPPIANS 4:6-7,9

By him therefore let us offer the sacrifice of praise to God continually, that is, the fruit of our lips giving thanks to his name.
HEBREWS 13:15

When You Need Physical Healing

YOUR PERSONAL NEEDS

Bless the Lord, O my soul, and forget not all his benefits:
Who forgiveth all thine iniquities; who healeth all thy
diseases.
PSALM 103:2-3

Surely he hath borne our griefs, and carried our sorrows:
yet we did esteem him stricken, smitten of God, and
afflicted.
But he was wounded for our transgressions, he was bruised
for our iniquities: the chastisement of our peace was upon
him; and with his stripes we are healed.
ISAIAH 53:4-5

For I will restore health unto thee, and I will heal thee
of thy wounds, saith the Lord;
JEREMIAH 30:17A

And when the woman saw that she was not hid, she came trembling, and falling down before him, she declared unto him before all the people for what cause she had touched him, and how she was healed immediately.
LUKE 8:47

And, behold, there was a woman which had a spirit of infirmity eighteen years, and was bowed together, and could in no wise lift up herself.
LUKE 13:11

And when Jesus saw her, he called her to him, and said unto her, Woman, thou art loosed from thine infirmity.
LUKE 8:47

And Jesus saith unto him, I will come and heal him.
MATTHEW 8:7

Is any among you afflicted? let him pray. Is any merry? let him sing psalms.
Is any sick among you? let him call for the elders of the church; and let them pray over him, anointing him with oil in the name of the Lord:
And the prayer of faith shall save the sick, and the Lord shall raise him up; and if he have committed sins, they shall be forgiven him.
Confess your faults one to another, and pray one for another, that ye may be healed. The effectual fervent prayer of a righteous man availeth much.
JAMES 5:13-16

When You Need Discernment

But there is a spirit in man: and the inspiration of the
Almighty giveth them understanding.
JOB 32:8

Counsel is mine, and sound wisdom: I am understanding;
I have strength.
PROVERBS 8:14

I will bless the Lord, who hath given me counsel: my reins
also instruct me in the night seasons.
PSALM 16:7

As for God, his way is perfect: the word of the Lord is
tried: he is a buckler to all those that trust in him.
PSALM 18:30

Teach me thy way, O Lord, and lead me in a plain path,
because of mine enemies.
PSALM 27:11

O send out thy light and thy truth: let them lead me; let
them bring me unto thy holy hill, and to thy tabernacles.
PSALM 43:3

The Lord will perfect that which concerneth me: thy mercy, O Lord, endureth forever: forsake not the works of thine own hands.
PSALM 138:8

Trust in the Lord with all thine heart; and lean not unto thine own understanding. In all thy ways acknowledge him, and he shall direct thy paths.
PROVERBS 3:5-6

Understanding is a wellspring of life unto him that hath it: but the instruction of fools is folly.
The heart of the wise teacheth his mouth, and addeth learning to his lips.
PROVERBS 16:22-23

Through wisdom is an house builded; and by understanding it is established: And by knowledge shall the chambers be filled with all precious and pleasant riches.
PROVERBS 24:3-4

For my thoughts are not your thoughts, neither are your ways my ways, saith the Lord. For as the heavens are higher than the earth, so are my ways higher than your ways, and my thoughts than your thoughts.
ISAIAH 55:8-9

Call unto me, and I will answer thee, and shew thee great and mighty things, which thou knowest not.
JEREMIAH 33:3

Then opened he their understanding, that they might understand the scriptures.
LUKE 24:45

When You Need Wisdom

I will bless the Lord, who hath given me counsel: my reins
also instruct me in the night seasons.
PSALM 16:7

Send out thy light and thy truth: let them lead me; let
them bring me unto thy holy hill, and to thy tabernacles.
PSALM 43:3

So teach us to number our days, that we may apply our
hearts unto wisdom.
PSALM 90:12

I am thy servant; give me understanding, that I may know
thy testimonies.
The entrance of thy words giveth light; it giveth understanding unto the simple.
PSALM 119:125,130

For the Lord giveth wisdom: out of his mouth cometh knowledge and understanding.He layeth up sound wisdom for the righteous: he is a buckler to them that walk uprightly.
PROVERBS 2:6-7

Trust in the Lord with all thine heart; and lean not unto thine own understanding. In all thy ways acknowledge him, and he shall direct thy paths.
PROVERBS 3:5-6

Whoso loveth instruction loveth knowledge: but he that hateth reproof is brutish.
PROVERBS 12:1

For God giveth to a man that is good in his sight wisdom, and knowledge, and joy: but to the sinner he giveth travail, to gather and to heap up, that he may give to him that is good before God. This also is vanity and vexation of spirit.
ECCLESIASTES 2:26

And thine ears shall hear a word behind thee, saying, This is the way, walk ye in it, when ye turn to the right hand, and when ye turn to the left.
ISAIAH 30:21

For to one is given by the Spirit the word of wisdom; to another the word of knowledge by the same Spirit.
1 CORINTHIANS 12:8

Cease not to give thanks for you, making mention of you
in my prayers; That the God of our Lord Jesus Christ,
the Father of glory, may give unto you the spirit of wisdom and revelation in the knowledge of him:
The eyes of your understanding being enlightened; that
ye may know what is the hope of his calling, and what
the riches of the glory of his inheritance in the saints,
EPHESIANS 1:16-18

For this cause we also, since the day we heard it, do not
cease to pray for you, and to desire that ye might be filled
with the knowledge of his will in all wisdom and spiritual
understanding;
That ye might walk worthy of the Lord unto all pleasing,
being fruitful in every good work, and increasing in the
knowledge of God.
COLOSSIANS 1:9-10

If any of you lack wisdom, let him ask of God, that giveth
to all men liberally, and upbraideth not; and it shall be
given him.
JAMES 1:5

For I will give you a mouth and wisdom, which all your
adversaries shall not be able to gainsay nor resist.
LUKE 21:15

Teach me thy way, O Lord, and lead me in a plain path, because of mine enemies.

PSALM 27:11

When You Feel Inadequate

YOUR PERSONAL NEEDS

For the Lord thy God is a merciful God; he will not forsake thee, neither destroy thee, nor forget the covenant of thy fathers which he sware unto them.
DEUTERONOMY 4:31

But thou, O Lord, art a shield for me; my glory, and the lifter up of mine head.
PSALM 3:3

I will not leave you comfortless: I will come to you.
JOHN 14:18

My voice shalt thou hear in the morning, O Lord; in the morning will I direct my prayer unto thee, and will look up.
PSALM 5:3

Though an host should encamp against me, my heart shall not fear: though war should rise against me, in this will I be confident.
For in the time of trouble he shall hide me in his pavilion: in the secret of his tabernacle shall he hide me; he shall set me up upon a rock.
PSALM 27:3,5

It is better to trust in the Lord than to put confidence in
man.
PSALM 118:8

He giveth power to the faint; and to them that have no
might he increaseth strength.
But they that wait upon the Lord shall renew their
strength; they shall mount up with wings as eagles; they
shall run, and not be weary; and they shall walk, and not
faint.
ISAIAH 40:29,31

Fear thou not; for I am with thee: be not dismayed; for I
am thy God: I will strengthen thee; yea, I will help thee;
yea, I will uphold thee with the right hand of my righteousness.
ISAIAH 41:10

When thou passest through the waters, I will be with
thee; and through the rivers, they shall not overflow thee:
when thou walkest through the fire, thou shalt not be
burned; neither shall the flame kindle upon thee.
ISAIAH 43:2

Wherein ye greatly rejoice, though now for a season, if
need be, ye are in heaviness through manifold temptations:
That the trial of your faith, being much more precious
than of gold that perisheth, though it be tried with fire,
might be found unto praise and honour and glory at the
appearing of Jesus Christ: Whom having not seen, ye
love; in whom, though now ye see him not, yet believing,
ye rejoice with joy unspeakable and full of glory: Receiving
the end of your faith, even the salvation of your souls.
1 PETER 1:6-9

When You Feel Physically Unattractive

For the Lord taketh pleasure in his people: he will beautify
the meek with salvation.

PSALM 149:4

A merry heart maketh a cheerful countenance: but by
sorrow of the heart the spirit is broken.

PROVERBS 15:13

But they that wait upon the Lord shall renew their
strength; they shall mount up with wings as eagles; they
shall run, and not be weary; and they shall walk, and not
faint.

ISAIAH 40:31

No weapon that is formed against thee shall prosper; and every tongue that shall rise against thee in judgment thou shalt condemn. This is the heritage of the servants of the Lord, and their righteousness is of me, saith the Lord.
ISAIAH 54:17

Judge not according to the appearance, but judge righteous judgment.
JOHN 7:24

Do ye look on things after the outward appearance? If any man trust to himself that he is Christ's, let him of himself think this again, that, as he is Christ's, even so are we Christ's.
2 CORINTHIANS 10:7

Being confident of this very thing, that he which hath begun a good work in you will perform it until the day of Jesus Christ.
PHILIPPIANS 1:6

And have put on the new man, which is renewed in knowledge after the image of him that created him.
COLOSSIANS 3:10

Now the God of peace, that brought again from the dead
our Lord Jesus, that great shepherd of the sheep, through
the blood of the everlasting covenant,
Make you perfect in every good work to do his will,
working in you that which is well-pleasing in his sight,
through Jesus Christ; to whom be glory for ever and ever.
Amen.
HEBREWS 13:20-21

Whose adorning let it not be that outward adorning of
plaiting the hair, and of wearing of gold, or of putting
on of apparel;
But let it be the hidden man of the heart, in that which
is not corruptible, even the ornament of a meek and quiet
spirit, which is in the sight of God of great price.
1 PETER 3:3-4

Let this mind be in you, which was also in Christ Jesus.
PHILIPPIANS 2:5

It is God that girdeth me with strength, and maketh my
way perfect.
PSALM 18:32

Favour is deceitful, and beauty is vain: but a woman that feareth the Lord, she shall be praised.

When You Face Sexual Temptation

But thou, O Lord, art a shield for me; my glory, and the lifter up of mine head.
PSALM 3:3

It is better to trust in the Lord than to put confidence in man.
PSALM 118:8

The Lord is my light and my salvation; whom shall I fear? the Lord is the strength of my life; of whom shall I be afraid?
Though an host should encamp against me, my heart shall not fear: though war should rise against me, in this will I be confident.
For in the time of trouble he shall hide me in his pavilion: in the secret of his tabernacle shall he hide me; he shall set me up upon a rock.
PSALM 27:1,3,5

Be pleased, O Lord, to deliver me: O Lord, make haste to help me. Let them be ashamed and confounded together that seek after my soul to destroy it; let them be driven backward and put to shame that wish me evil.
PSALM 40:13-14

Thy word have I hid in mine heart, that I might not sin
against thee.
PSALM 119:11

For the Lord shall be thy confidence, and shall keep thy
foot from being taken.
PROVERBS 3:26

Let thine eyes look right on, and let thine eyelids look
straight before thee.
Turn not to the right hand nor to the left: remove thy
foot from evil.
PROVERBS 4:25,27

The way of the Lord is strength to the upright: but
destruction shall be to the workers of iniquity.
PROVERBS 10:29

In the fear of the Lord is strong confidence: and his
children shall have a place of refuge.
PROVERBS 14:26

He that covereth his sins shall not prosper: but whoso
confesseth and forsaketh them shall have mercy.
PROVERBS 28:13

He giveth power to the faint; and to them that have no
might he increaseth strength.
ISAIAH 40:29

Fear thou not; for I am with thee: be not dismayed; for I am thy God: I will strengthen thee; yea, I will help thee; yea, I will uphold thee with the right hand of my righteousness.
ISAIAH 41:10

And lead us not into temptation, but deliver us from evil: For thine is the kingdom, and the power, and the glory, for ever. Amen.
MATTHEW 6:13

For sin shall not have dominion over you: for ye are not under the law, but under grace.
ROMANS 6:14

There hath no temptation taken you but such as is common to man: but God is faithful, who will not suffer you to be tempted above that ye are able; but will with the temptation also make a way to escape, that ye may be able to bear it.
1 CORINTHIANS 10:13

And my temptation which was in my flesh ye despised not, nor rejected; but received me as an angel of God, even as Christ Jesus.
GALATIANS 4:14

Let no man say when he is tempted, I am tempted of God: for God cannot be tempted with evil, neither tempteth he any man:
But every man is tempted, when he is drawn away of his own lust, and enticed.
JAMES 1:13-14

Watch and pray, that ye enter not into temptation: the spirit indeed is willing, but the flesh is weak.

MATTHEW 26:41

Be sober, be vigilant; because your adversary the devil, as a roaring lion, walketh about, seeking whom he may devour: Whom resist stedfast in the faith, knowing that the same afflictions are accomplished in your brethren that are in the world.

1 PETER 5:8-9

The Lord knoweth how to deliver the godly out of temptations, and to reserve the unjust unto the day of judgment to be punished:

2 PETER 2:9

Because thou hast kept the word of my patience, I also will keep thee from the hour of temptation, which shall come upon all the world, to try them that dwell upon the earth.

REVELATION 3:10

When You Feel Angry or Resentful

YOUR PERSONAL NEEDS

I will bless the Lord, who hath given me counsel: my reins
also instruct me in the night seasons.
I have set the Lord always before me: because he is at my
right hand, I shall not be moved.
Therefore my heart is glad, and my glory rejoiceth: my
flesh also shall rest in hope.

PSALM 16:7-9

Cease from anger, and forsake wrath: fret not thyself in
any wise to do evil.

PSALM 37:8

Behold, thou desirest truth in the inward parts: and in
the hidden part thou shalt make me to know wisdom.
Create in me a clean heart, O God; and renew a right spirit
within me.

PSALM 51:6,10

In God I will praise his word, in God I have put my trust;
I will not fear what flesh can do unto me.

PSALM 56:4

Teach me thy way, O Lord; I will walk in thy truth: unite
my heart to fear thy name.
PSALM 86:11

Trust in the Lord with all thine heart; and lean not unto
thine own understanding. In all thy ways acknowledge
him, and he shall direct thy paths.
For the Lord shall be thy confidence.
PROVERBS 3:5-6,26A

He that is slow to anger is better than the mighty; and
he that ruleth his spirit than he that taketh a city.
PROVERBS 16:32

The fear of man bringeth a snare: but whoso putteth his
trust in the Lord shall be safe.
PROVERBS 29:25

Be not hasty in thy spirit to be angry: for anger resteth
in the bosom of fools.
ECCLESIASTES 7:9

Behold, God is my salvation; I will trust, and not be afraid:
for the Lord Jehovah is my strength and my song; he also
is become my salvation.
ISAIAH 12:2

Blessed are the peacemakers: for they shall be called the
children of God.
MATTHEW 5:9

Charity suffereth long, and is kind; charity envieth not;
charity vaunteth not itself, is not puffed up,
Doth not behave itself unseemly, seeketh not her own, is
not easily provoked, thinketh no evil.
1 CORINTHIANS 13:4-5

For the weapons of our warfare are not carnal, but mighty
through God to the pulling down of strong holds.
2 CORINTHIANS 10:4

But the fruit of the Spirit is love, joy, peace, long-suffering,
gentleness, goodness, faith, meekness, temperance: against
such there is no law.
GALATIANS 5:22-23

He that descended is the same also that ascended up far
above all heavens, that he might fill all things.
EPHESIANS 4:10

Finally, my brethren, be strong in the Lord, and in the
power of his might.
EPHESIANS 6:10

He that is soon angry dealeth foolishly: and a man of wicked devices is hated.

PROVERBS 14:17

Finally, brethren, whatsoever things are true, whatsoever things are honest, whatsoever things are just, whatsoever things are pure, whatsoever things are lovely, whatsoever things are of good report; if there be any virtue, and if there be any praise, think on these things.

PHILIPPIANS 4:8

Beloved, think it not strange concerning the fiery trial which is to try you, as though some strange thing happened unto you.

1 PETER 4:12

When You Feel Lonely and Unappreciated

YOUR PERSONAL NEEDS

Be strong and of a good courage, fear not, nor be afraid of them: for the Lord thy God, he it is that doth go with thee; he will not fail thee, nor forsake thee.
DEUTERONOMY 31:6

For the Lord will not forsake his people for his great name's sake: because it hath pleased the Lord to make you his people.
1 SAMUEL 12:22

Casting all your care upon him; for he careth for you.
1 PETER 5:7

And they that know thy name will put their trust in thee: for thou, Lord, hast not forsaken them that seek thee.
PSALM 9:10

As for God, his way is perfect: the word of the Lord is tried: he is a buckler to all those that trust in him.
PSALM 18:30

The Lord hear thee in the day of trouble; the name of the God of Jacob defend thee; Send thee help from the sanctuary, and strengthen thee out of Zion.
PSALM 20:1-2

Yea, though I walk through the valley of the shadow of death, I will fear no evil: for thou art with me; thy rod and thy staff they comfort me.
PSALM 23:4

Many are the afflictions of the righteous: but the Lord delivereth him out of them all.
PSALM 34:19

Why art thou cast down, O my soul? and why art thou disquieted within me? hope in God: for I shall yet praise him, who is the health of my countenance, and my God.
PSALM 43:5

My soul, wait thou only upon God; for my expectation is from him.
PSALM 62:5

Because he hath set his love upon me, therefore will I deliver him: I will set him on high, because he hath known my name. He shall call upon me, and I will answer him: I will be with him in trouble; I will deliver him, and honour him.
PSALM 91:14-15

Keep thy heart with all diligence; for out of it are the issues of life.
PROVERBS 4:23

The eyes of all wait upon thee; and thou givest them their meat in due season. Thou openest thine hand, and satisfiest the desire of every living thing.
PSALM 145:15-16

Trust in the Lord with all thine heart; and lean not unto thine own understanding. In all thy ways acknowledge him, and he shall direct thy paths.
PROVERBS 3:5-6

Fear thou not; for I am with thee: be not dismayed; for I am thy God: I will strengthen thee; yea, I will help thee; yea, I will uphold thee with the right hand of my right-eousness.
ISAIAH 41:10

For thou hast been a strength to the poor, a strength to the needy in his distress, a refuge from the storm, a shadow from the heat, when the blast of the terrible ones is as a storm against the wall.
ISAIAH 25:4

Can a woman forget her sucking child, that she should not have compassion on the son of her womb? yea, they may forget, yet will I not forget thee.
Behold, I have graven thee upon the palms of my hands; thy walls are continually before me.
ISAIAH 49:15-16

Teaching them to observe all things whatsoever I have commanded you: and, lo, I am with you alway, even unto the end of the world. Amen.
MATTHEW 28:20

I wait for the Lord, my soul doth wait, and in his word do I hope.

PSALM 130:5

Behold, I give unto you power to tread on serpents and scorpions, and over all the power of the enemy: and nothing shall by any means hurt you.
LUKE 10:19

What shall we then say to these things? If God be for us, who can be against us?
ROMANS 8:31

So that we may boldly say, The Lord is my helper, and I will not fear what man shall do unto me.
HEBREWS 13:6

And they overcame him by the blood of the Lamb, and by the word of their testimony; and they loved not their lives unto the death.
REVELATION 12:11

When You Need Ability

I can do all things through Christ which strengtheneth me.
PHILIPPIANS 4:13

Forasmuch as ye are manifestly declared to be the epistle
of Christ ministered by us, written not with ink, but with
the Spirit of the living God; not in tables of stone, but
in fleshy tables of the heart.
And such trust have we through Christ to God-ward.
2 CORINTHIANS 3:3-4

I thank my God always on your behalf, for the grace of
God which is given you by Jesus Christ;
That in every thing ye are enriched by him, in all utterance,
and in all knowledge;
Even as the testimony of Christ was confirmed in you:
So that ye come behind in no gift; waiting for the coming
of our Lord Jesus Christ.
1 CORINTHIANS 1:4-7

As every man hath received the gift, even so minister the same one to another, as good stewards of the manifold grace of God.
If any man speak, let him speak as the oracles of God; if any man minister, let him do it as of the ability which God giveth: that God in all things may be glorified through Jesus Christ, to whom be praise and dominion for ever and ever. Amen.

1 PETER 4:10-11

And I have filled him with the spirit of God, in wisdom, and in understanding, and in knowledge, and in all manner of workmanship.

EXODUS 31:3

And I, behold, I have given with him Aholiab, the son of Ahisamach, of the tribe of Dan: and in the hearts of all that are wise hearted I have put wisdom, that they may make all that I have commanded thee.

EXODUS 31:6

Grace and peace be multiplied unto you through the knowledge of God, and of Jesus our Lord,
According as his divine power hath given unto us all things that pertain unto life and godliness, through the knowledge of him that hath called us to glory and virtue.

2 PETER 1:2-3

Blessed be the Lord my strength, which teacheth my
hands to war, and my fingers to fight.
PSALM 144:1

Abide in me, and I in you. As the branch cannot bear fruit
of itself, except it abide in the vine; no more can ye, except
ye abide in me.
I am the vine, ye are the branches: He that abideth in me,
and I in him, the same bringeth forth much fruit: for
without me ye can do nothing.
JOHN 15:4-5

If ye abide in me, and my words abide in you, ye shall ask
what ye will, and it shall be done unto you.
JOHN 15:7

For by thee I have run through a troop; and by my God
have I leaped over a wall.
PSALM 18:29

But my God shall supply all your need according to his
riches in glory by Christ Jesus.
PHILIPPIANS 4:19

Nay, in all these things we are more than conquerors through him that loved us.

ROMANS 8:37

When You Need a Friend

Thou art my hiding place; thou shalt preserve me from trouble; thou shalt compass me about with songs of deliverance.

PSALM 32:7

He shall call upon me, and I will answer him: I will be with him in trouble; I will deliver him, and honour him.

PSALM 91:15

A man that hath friends must shew himself friendly: and there is a friend that sticketh closer than a brother.

PROVERBS 18:24

He that walketh with wise men shall be wise: but a companion of fools shall be destroyed.

PROVERBS 13:20

Let nothing be done through strife or vainglory; but in lowliness of mind let each esteem other better than themselves. Look not every man on his own things, but every man also on the things of others.
PHILIPPIANS 2:3-4

For the Lord God is a sun and shield: the Lord will give grace and glory: no good thing will he withhold from them that walk uprightly.
PSALM 84:11

Delight thyself also in the Lord; and he shall give thee the desires of thine heart.
Whither shall I go from thy spirit? or whither shall I flee from thy presence?
PSALM 139:7

Even there shall thy hand lead me, and thy right hand shall hold me.
PSALM 139:10

A friend loveth at all times, and a brother is born for adversity.
PROVERBS 17:17

When You Need Encouragement

In the day when I cried thou answeredst me, and strength-
enedst me with strength in my soul.
PSALM 138:3

Though I walk in the midst of trouble, thou wilt revive
me: thou shalt stretch forth thine hand against the wrath
of mine enemies, and thy right hand shall save me. The
Lord will perfect that which concerneth me: thy mercy,
O Lord, endureth for ever: forsake not the works of thine
own hands.
PSALM 138:7-8

But the path of the just is as the shining light, that shineth
more and more unto the perfect day.
PROVERBS 4:18

But thou, O Lord, be merciful unto me, and raise me up,
that I may requite them.
PSALM 41:10

When thou passest through the waters, I will be with
thee; and through the rivers, they shall not overflow thee:
when thou walkest through the fire, thou shalt not be
burned; neither shall the flame kindle upon thee.
ISAIAH 43:2

The humble shall see this, and be glad: and your heart
shall live that seek God.
PSALM 69:32

For the Lord shall comfort Zion: he will comfort all her
waste places; and he will make her wilderness like Eden,
and her desert like the garden of the Lord; joy and gladness shall be found therein, thanksgiving, and the voice
of melody.
ISAIAH 51:3

I, even I, am he that comforteth you: who art thou, that
thou shouldest be afraid of a man that shall die, and of
the son of man which shall be made as grass.
ISAIAH 51:12

The Lord will perfect that which concerneth me: thy
mercy, O Lord, endureth for ever: forsake not the works
of thine own hands.
PSALM 138:8

Now our Lord Jesus Christ himself, and God, even our
Father, which hath loved us, and hath given us everlasting
consolation and good hope through grace,
Comfort your hearts, and stablish you in every good word
and work.
2 THESSALONIANS 2:16-17

For God is not unrighteous to forget your work and labour
of love, which ye have shewed toward his name, in that
ye have ministered to the saints, and do minister.
And we desire that every one of you do shew the same
diligence to the full assurance of hope unto the end:
That ye be not slothful, but followers of them who through
faith and patience inherit the promises.
HEBREWS 6:10-12

But the mercy of the Lord is from everlasting to everlasting upon them that fear him, and his righteousness unto children's children.
PSALM 103:17

For I know the thoughts that I think toward you, saith the Lord, thoughts of peace, and not of evil, to give you an expected end.
JEREMIAH 29:11

Be strong and of a good courage, fear not, nor be afraid of them: for the Lord thy God, he it is that doth go with thee; he will not fail thee, nor forsake thee.
DEUTERONOMY 31:6

Nevertheless I am continually with thee: thou hast holden me by my right hand.
PSALM 73:23

Have not I commanded thee? Be strong and of a good courage; be not afraid, neither be thou dismayed: for the Lord thy God is with thee whithersoever thou goest.
JOSHUA 1:9

Then he answered and spake unto me, saying, This is the word of the Lord unto Zerubbabel, saying, Not by might, nor by power, but by my spirit, saith the Lord of hosts.
ZECHARIAH 4:6

Now thanks be unto God, which always causeth us to triumph in Christ, and maketh manifest the savour of his knowledge by us in every place.
2 CORINTHIANS 2:14

Being confident of this very thing, that he which hath begun a good work in you will perform it until the day of Jesus Christ.

PHILIPPIANS 1:6

Trust in the Lord, and do good; so shalt thou dwell in the land, and verily thou shalt be fed. Delight thyself also in the Lord; and he shall give thee the desires of thine heart. Commit thy way unto the Lord; trust also in him; and he shall bring it to pass.
PSALM 37:3-5

O bless our God, ye people, and make the voice of his praise to be heard: Which holdeth our soul in life, and suffereth not our feet to be moved.
PSALM 66:8-9

I will praise the name of God with a song, and will magnify him with thanksgiving.
PSALM 69:30

When You Need Faith

The Lord is my shepherd; I shall not want.
PSALM 23:1

But what saith it? The word is nigh thee, even in thy mouth, and in thy heart: that is, the word of faith, which we preach.
ROMANS 10:8

As for God, his way is perfect; the word of the Lord is tried: he is a buckler to all them that trust in him.
2 SAMUEL 22:31

The Lord also will be a refuge for the oppressed, a refuge in times of trouble. And they that know thy name will put their trust in thee: for thou, Lord, hast not forsaken them that seek thee.
PSALM 9:9-10

Fear not, O land; be glad and rejoice: for the Lord will do great things.
JOEL 2:21

It is better to trust in the Lord than to put confidence in man. It is better to trust in the Lord than to put confidence in princes.
PSALM 118:8-9

They that trust in the Lord shall be as mount Zion, which cannot be removed, but abideth for ever.
PSALM 125:1

My help cometh from the Lord, which made heaven and earth. He will not suffer thy foot to be moved: he that keepeth thee will not slumber. Behold, he that keepeth Israel shall neither slumber nor sleep.
PSALM 121:2-4

But let all those that put their trust in thee rejoice: let them ever shout for joy, because thou defendest them: let them also that love thy name be joyful in thee.
PSALM 5:11

Now the God of hope fill you with all joy and peace in believing, that ye may abound in hope, through the power of the Holy Ghost.
ROMANS 15:13

For this cause also thank we God without ceasing, because, when ye received the word of God which ye heard of us, ye received it not as the word of men, but as it is in truth, the word of God, which effectually worketh also in you that believe.
1 THESSALONIANS 2:13

Now the just shall live by faith: but if any man draw back,
my soul shall have no pleasure in him.
But we are not of them who draw back unto perdition;
but of them that believe to the saving of the soul.
HEBREWS 10:38-39

For whatsoever is born of God overcometh the world:
and this is the victory that overcometh the world, even
our faith.
1 JOHN 5:4

And the Lord, he it is that doth go before thee; he will be
with thee, he will not fail thee, neither forsake thee: fear
not, neither be dismayed.
DEUTERONOMY 31:8

And they rose early in the morning, and went forth into
the wilderness of Tekoa: and as they went forth, Je-
hoshaphat stood and said, Hear me, O Judah, and ye
inhabitants of Jerusalem; Believe in the Lord your God,
so shall ye be established; believe his prophets, so shall ye
prosper.
2 CHRONICLES 20:20

Be strong and courageous, be not afraid nor dismayed for
the king of Assyria, nor for all the multitude that is with
him: for there be more with us than with him:
With him is an arm of flesh; but with us is the Lord our
God to help us, and to fight our battles. And the people
rested themselves upon the words of Hezekiah king of
Judah.
2 CHRONICLES 32:7-8

So then faith cometh by hearing, and hearing by the word of God.

ROMANS 10:17

But in those sacrifices there is a remembrance again made
of sins every year.
HEBREWS 10:3

Behold, his soul which is lifted up is not upright in him:
but the just shall live by his faith.
HABAKKUK 2:4

And David said to Solomon his son, Be strong and of
good courage, and do it: fear not, nor be dismayed: for the
Lord God, even my God, will be with thee; he will not
fail thee, nor forsake thee, until thou hast finished all the
work for the service of the house of the Lord.
1 CHRONICLES 28:20

When You Need Joy

For ye were sometimes darkness, but now are ye light in
the Lord: walk as children of light.
EPHESIANS 5:8

Thou wilt shew me the path of life: in thy presence is
fulness of joy; at thy right hand there are pleasures for
evermore.
PSALM 16:11

Glory and honour are in his presence; strength and
gladness are in his place.
1 CHRONICLES 16:27

Also that day they offered great sacrifices, and rejoiced:
for God had made them rejoice with great joy: the wives
also and the children rejoiced: so that the joy of Jerusalem
was heard even afar off.
NEHEMIAH 12:43

Thou hast put gladness in my heart, more than in the
time that their com and their wine increased.
PSALM 4:7

I will be glad and rejoice in thee: I will sing praise to thy
name, O thou most High.
PSALM 9:2

The statutes of the Lord are right, rejoicing the heart:
the commandment of the Lord is pure, enlightening the eyes.
PSALM 19:8

The Lord is my strength and my shield; my heart trusted
in him, and I am helped: therefore my heart greatly rejoiceth; and with my song will I praise him.
PSALM 28:7

And my soul shall be joyful in the Lord: it shall rejoice in
his salvation.
PSALM 35:9

Wilt thou not revive us again: that thy people may rejoice
in thee?
PSALM 85:6

Those things, which ye have both learned, and received,
and heard, and seen in me, do: and the God of peace shall
be with you.
PHILIPPIANS 4:9

Blessed is the people that know the joyful sound: they
shall walk, O Lord, in the light of thy countenance.
In thy name shall they rejoice all the day: and in thy
righteousness shall they be exalted.
PSALM 89:15-16

Make a joyful noise unto the Lord, all ye lands.
Serve the Lord with gladness: come before his presence
with singing.
PSALM 100:1-2

When the Lord turned again the captivity of Zion, we were like them that dream. Then was our mouth filled with laughter, and our tongue with singing: then said they among the heathen, The Lord hath done great things for them.
PSALM 126:1-2

Thy words were found, and I did eat them; and thy word was unto me the joy and rejoicing of mine heart: for I am called by thy name, O Lord God of hosts.
JEREMIAH 15:16

Notwithstanding in this rejoice not, that the spirits are subject unto you; but rather rejoice, because your names are written in heaven.
LUKE 10:20

These things have I spoken unto you, that my joy might remain in you, and that your joy might be full.
JOHN 15:11

Thou hast made known to me the ways of life; thou shalt make me full of joy with thy countenance.
ACTS 2:28

And the disciples were filled with joy, and with the Holy Ghost.
ACTS 13:52

For the kingdom of God is not meat and drink; but righteousness, and peace, and joy in the Holy Ghost.
ROMANS 14:17

Whom having not seen, ye love; in whom, though now ye see him not, yet believing, ye rejoice with joy unspeakable and full of glory.

1 PETER 1:8

When You Need Love

And hope maketh not ashamed; because the love of God
is shed abroad in our hearts by the Holy Ghost which is
given unto us.
ROMANS 5:5

And this I pray, that your love may abound yet more and
more in knowledge and in all judgment;
That ye may approve things that are excellent; that ye
may be sincere and without offence till the day of Christ;
Being filled with the fruits of righteousness, which are
by Jesus Christ, unto the glory and praise of God.
PHILIPPIANS 1:9-11

And the Lord make you to increase and abound in love
one toward another, and toward all men, even as we do
toward you: To the end he may stablish your hearts un-
blameable in holiness before God, even our Father, at the
coming of our Lord Jesus Christ with all his saints.
1 THESSALONIANS 3:12-13

But as touching brotherly love ye need not that I write unto you: for ye yourselves are taught of God to love one another. And indeed ye do it toward all the brethren which are in all Macedonia: but we beseech you, brethren, that ye increase more and more.
1 THESSALONIANS 4:9-10

And the Lord direct your hearts into the love of God, and into the patient waiting for Christ.
2 THESSALONIANS 3:5

Herein is love, not that we loved God, but that he loved us, and sent his Son to be the propitiation for our sins. Beloved, if God so loved us, we ought also to love one another. No man hath seen God at any time. If we love one another, God dwelleth in us, and his love is perfected in us.
1 JOHN 4:10-12

And we have known and believed the love that God hath to us. God is love; and he that dwelleth in love dwelleth in God, and God in him. Herein is our love made perfect, that we may have boldness in the day of judgment: because as he is, so are we in this world. There is no fear in love; but perfect love casteth out fear: because fear hath torment. He that feareth is not made perfect in love.
1 JOHN 4:16-18

Desiring to be teachers of the law; understanding neither what they say, nor whereof they affirm.
1 TIMOTHY 1:7

Hatred stirreth up strifes: but love covereth all sins.
PROVERBS 10:12

Set me as a seal upon thine heart, as a seal upon thine arm: for love is strong as death; jealousy is cruel as the grave: the coals thereof are coals of fire, which hath a most vehement flame.
Many waters cannot quench love, neither can the floods drown it: if a man would give all the substance of his house for love, it would utterly be contemned.
SONG OF SOLOMON 8:6-7

He that covereth a transgression seeketh love; but he that repeateth a matter separateth very friends.
PROVERBS 17:9

A friend loveth at all times, and a brother is born for adversity.
PROVERBS 17:17

Honour thy father and thy mother: and, Thou shalt love thy neighbour as thyself.
MATTHEW 19:19

And thou shalt love the Lord thy God with all thine heart, and with all thy soul, and with all thy might.
DEUTERONOMY 6:5

And now, Israel, what doth the Lord thy God require of thee, but to fear the Lord thy God, to walk in all his ways, and to love him, and to serve the Lord thy God with all thy heart and with all thy soul.
DEUTERONOMY 10:12

And above all things have fervent charity among yourselves: for charity shall cover the multitude of sins.

1 PETER 4:8

And I made an ark of shittim wood, and hewed two tables of stone like unto the first, and went up into the mount, having the two tables in mine hand.

DEUTERONOMY 10:3

But take diligent heed to do the commandment and the law, which Moses the servant of the Lord charged you, to love the Lord your God, and to walk in all his ways, and to keep his commandments, and to cleave unto him, and to serve him with all your heart and with all your soul.

JOSHUA 22:5

I love the Lord, because he hath heard my voice and my supplications.

PSALM 116:1

And Jesus answered and said unto them, I will also ask of you one question, and answer me, and I will tell you by what authority I do these things. The baptism of John, was it from heaven, or of men? answer me.
And they reasoned with themselves, saying, If we shall say, From heaven; he will say, Why then did ye not believe him?
But if we shall say, Of men; they feared the people: for all men counted John, that he was a prophet indeed.
And they answered and said unto Jesus, We cannot tell. And Jesus answering saith unto them, Neither do I tell you by what authority I do these things.
MARK 11:29-33

A new commandment I give unto you, That ye love one another; as I have loved you, that ye also love one another. By this shall all men know that ye are my disciples, if ye have love one to another.
JOHN 13:34-35

Now as touching things offered unto idols, we know that we all have knowledge. Knowledge puffeth up, but charity edifieth.
1 CORINTHIANS 8:1

Now the end of the commandment is charity out of a pure heart, and of a good conscience, and of faith unfeigned.
1 TIMOTHY 1:5

He that loveth
his brother
abideth in the
light, and there
is none occasion
of stumbling in
him.

---

1 JOHN 2:10

When You Need Motivation

Servants, obey in all things your masters according to
the flesh; not with eye-service, as men-pleasers; but in
singleness of heart, fearing God:
And whatsoever ye do, do it heartily, as to the Lord, and
not unto men.
COLOSSIANS 3:22-23

And in the same house remain, eating and drinking such
things as they give: for the labourer is worthy of his hire.
Go not from house to house.
LUKE 10:7

Wherefore I put thee in remembrance that thou stir up
the gift of God, which is in thee by the putting on of my
hands.For God hath not given us the spirit of fear; but
of power, and of love, and of a sound mind.
2 TIMOTHY 1:6-7

And the people the men of Israel encouraged themselves,
and set their battle again in array in the place where they
put themselves in array the first day.
JUDGES 20:22

He becometh poor that dealeth with a slack hand: but the
hand of the diligent maketh rich.
PROVERBS 10:4

The hand of the diligent shall bear rule: but the slothful
shall be under tribute.
PROVERBS 12:24

Seest thou a man diligent in his business? he shall stand
before kings; he shall not stand before mean men.
PROVERBS 22:29

I lead in the way of righteousness, in the midst of the
paths of judgment:
That I may cause those that love me to inherit substance;
and I will fill their treasures.
PROVERBS 8:20-21

Not slothful in business; fervent in spirit; serving the Lord.
ROMANS 12:11

Slothfulness casteth into a deep sleep; and an idle soul
shall suffer hunger.
PROVERBS 19:15

He that gathereth in summer is a wise son: but he that
sleepeth in harvest is a son that causeth shame.
PROVERBS 10:5

He that tilleth his land shall be satisfied with bread: but
he that followeth vain persons is void of understanding.
PROVERBS 12:11

Wealth gotten by vanity shall be diminished: but he that
gathereth by labour shall increase.
PROVERBS 13:11

Love not sleep, lest thou come to poverty; open thine eyes,
and thou shalt be satisfied with bread.
PROVERBS 20:13

And that ye study to be quiet, and to do your own business,
and to work with your own hands, as we commanded you;
That ye may walk honestly toward them that are without,
and that ye may have lack of nothing.
1 THESSALONIANS 4:11-12

For even when we were with you, this we commanded
you, that if any would not work, neither should he eat.
2 THESSALONIANS 3:10

That ye be not slothful, but followers of them who through
faith and patience inherit the promises.
HEBREWS 6:12

By much slothfulness the building decayeth; and through
idleness of the hands the house droppeth through.
ECCLESIASTES 10:18

Nay, in all these things we are more than conquerors through him that loved us.

ROMANS 8:37

When You Need Patience

Rest in the Lord, and wait patiently for him: fret not thyself because of him who prospereth in his way, because of the man who bringeth wicked devices to pass. Cease from anger, and forsake wrath: fret not thyself in any wise to do evil. For evildoers shall be cut off: but those that wait upon the Lord, they shall inherit the earth.

PSALM 37:7-9

Better is the end of a thing than the beginning thereof: and the patient in spirit is better than the proud in spirit. Be not hasty in thy spirit to be angry: for anger resteth in the bosom of fools.

ECCLESIASTES 7:8-9

In your patience possess ye your souls.

LUKE 21:19

And not only so, but we glory in tribulations also: knowing that tribulation worketh patience.

ROMANS 5:3

And let us not be weary in well doing: for in due season
we shall reap, if we faint not.
GALATIANS 6:9

I therefore, the prisoner of the Lord, beseech you that ye
walk worthy of the vocation wherewith ye are called.
EPHESIANS 4:1

With all lowliness and meekness, with long-suffering,
forbearing one another in love.
EPHESIANS 4:2

That ye might walk worthy of the Lord unto all pleasing,
being fruitful in every good work, and increasing in the
knowledge of God;
Strengthened with all might, according to his glorious
power, unto all patience and long-suffering with joyfulness.
COLOSSIANS 1:10-11

Now we exhort you, brethren, warn them that are unruly,
comfort the feebleminded, support the weak, be patient
toward all men.
1 THESSALONIANS 5:14

And the Lord direct your hearts into the love of God,
and into the patient waiting for Christ.
2 THESSALONIANS 3:5

But thou, O man of God, flee these things; and follow
after righteousness, godliness, faith, love, patience, meekness.
1 TIMOTHY 6:11

That ye be not slothful, but followers of them who through
faith and patience inherit the promises.
HEBREWS 6:12

For ye have need of patience, that, after ye have done the
will of God, ye might receive the promise.
HEBREWS 10:36

Wherefore seeing we also are compassed about with so
great a cloud of witnesses, let us lay aside every weight,
and the sin which doth so easily beset us, and let us run
with patience the race that is set before us.
HEBREWS 12:1

Knowing this, that the trying of your faith worketh
patience. But let patience have her perfect work, that ye
may be perfect and entire, wanting nothing.
JAMES 1:3-4

Wherefore, my beloved brethren, let every man be swift
to hear, slow to speak, slow to wrath.
JAMES 1:19

Be patient therefore, brethren, unto the coming of the
Lord. Behold, the husbandman waiteth for the precious
fruit of the earth, and hath long patience for it, until he
receive the early and latter rain. Be ye also patient; stablish
your hearts: for the coming of the Lord draweth nigh.
JAMES 5:7-8

And so, after he had patiently endured, he obtained the promise.

HEBREWS 6:15

And beside this, giving all diligence, add to your faith virtue; and to virtue knowledge; And to knowledge temperance; and to temperance patience; and to patience godliness.
2 PETER 1:5-6

Here is the patience of the saints: here are they that keep the commandments of God, and the faith of Jesus.
REVELATION 14:12

The Lord is not slack concerning his promise, as some men count slackness; but is long-suffering to us-ward, not willing that any should perish, but that all should come to repentance.
2 PETER 3:9

When You Need Protection

For this shall every one that is godly pray unto thee in a
time when thou mayest be found: surely in the floods of
great waters they shall not come nigh unto him.
Thou art my hiding place; thou shalt preserve me from
trouble; thou shalt compass me about with songs of deliverance.

PSALM 32:6-7

For I, saith the Lord, will be unto her a wall of fire round
about, and will be the glory in the midst of her.

ZECHARIAH 2:5

God is our refuge and strength, a very present help in
trouble. Therefore will not we fear, though the earth be
removed, and though the mountains be carried into the
midst of the sea.

PSALM 46:1-2

God is in the midst of her; she shall not be moved: God
shall help her, and that right early.

PSALM 46:5

He that dwelleth in the secret place of the most High
shall abide under the shadow of the Almighty.
I will say of the Lord, He is my refuge and my fortress:
my God; in him will I trust.
Surely he shall deliver thee from the snare of the fowler,
and from the noisome pestilence.
He shall cover thee with his feathers, and under his wings
shalt thou trust: his truth shall be thy shield and buckler.
Thou shalt not be afraid for the terror by night; nor for
the arrow that flieth by day;
Nor for the pestilence that walketh in darkness; nor for
the destruction that wasteth at noonday.
A thousand shall fall at thy side, and ten thousand at thy
right hand; but it shall not come nigh thee.
Only with thine eyes shalt thou behold and see the reward
of the wicked.
Because thou hast made the Lord, which is my refuge,
even the most High, thy habitation;
There shall no evil befall thee, neither shall any plague
come nigh thy dwelling.
For he shall give his angels charge over thee, to keep thee
in all thy ways.
They shall bear thee up in their hands, lest thou dash thy
foot against a stone.
Thou shalt tread upon the lion and adder: the young lion
and the dragon shalt thou trample under feet.
Because he hath set his love upon me, therefore will I
deliver him: I will set him on high, because he hath known
my name.
He shall call upon me, and I will answer him: I will be
with him in trouble; I will deliver him, and honour him.
With long life will I satisfy him, and shew him my salvation.

PSALM 91:1-16

What time I am afraid, I will trust in thee. In God I will praise his word, in God I have put my trust; I will not fear what flesh can do unto me.
PSALM 56:3-4

Give us help from trouble: for vain is the help of man. Through God we shall do valiantly: for he it is that shall tread down our enemies.
PSALM 60:11-12

Hear my cry, O God; attend unto my prayer.
From the end of the earth will I cry unto thee, when my heart is overwhelmed: lead me to the rock that is higher than I. For thou hast been a shelter for me, and a strong tower from the enemy. I will abide in thy tabernacle for ever: I will trust in the covert of thy wings.
PSALM 61:1-4

In the fear of the Lord is strong confidence: and his children shall have a place of refuge.
The fear of the Lord is a fountain of life, to depart from the snares of death.
PROVERBS 14:26-27

As for God, his way is perfect; the word of the Lord is tried: he is a buckler to all them that trust in him.
2 SAMUEL 22:31

For the which cause I also suffer these things: nevertheless I am not ashamed: for I know whom I have believed, and am persuaded that he is able to keep that which I have committed unto him against that day.
2 TIMOTHY 1:12

Now unto him that is able to keep you from falling, and to present you faultless before the presence of his glory with exceeding joy.

JUDE 1:24

When You Need Self-Control

But put ye on the Lord Jesus Christ, and make not provision for the flesh, to fulfill the lusts thereof.
ROMANS 13:14

Knowing this, that our old man is crucified with him, that the body of sin might be destroyed, that henceforth we should not serve sin.
ROMANS 6:6

And put a knife to thy throat, if thou be a man given to appetite.
PROVERBS 23:2

He that is slow to anger is better than the mighty; and he that ruleth his spirit than he that taketh a city.
PROVERBS 16:32

I am crucified with Christ: nevertheless I live; yet not I, but Christ liveth in me: and the life which I now live in the flesh I live by the faith of the Son of God, who loved me, and gave himself for me.
GALATIANS 2:20

This I say then, Walk in the Spirit, and ye shall not fulfill the lust of the flesh.
GALATIANS 5:16

No man that warreth entangleth himself with the affairs of this life; that he may please him who hath chosen him to be a soldier.
2 TIMOTHY 2:4

Forasmuch then as Christ hath suffered for us in the flesh, arm yourselves likewise with the same mind: for he that hath suffered in the flesh hath ceased from sin;
That he no longer should live the rest of his time in the flesh to the lusts of men, but to the will of God.
1 PETER 4:1-2

Hast thou found honey? eat so much as is sufficient for thee, lest thou be filled therewith, and vomit it.
PROVERBS 25:16

All things are lawful unto me, but all things are not expedient: all things are lawful for me, but I will not be brought under the power of any.
1 CORINTHIANS 6:12

And every man that striveth for the mastery is temperate in all things. Now they do it to obtain a corruptible crown; but we an incorruptible.
I therefore so run, not as uncertainly; so fight I, not as one that beateth the air: But I keep under my body, and bring it into subjection: lest that by any means, when I have preached to others, I myself should be a castaway.
1 CORINTHIANS 9:25-27

Let your moderation be known unto all men. The Lord is at hand.
PHILIPPIANS 4:5

And they that are Christ's have crucified the flesh with the affections and lusts.
GALATIANS 5:24

Dearly beloved, I beseech you as strangers and pilgrims, abstain from fleshly lusts, which war against the soul.

1 PETER 2:11

When You Feel Weak

The Lord is my strength and song, and he is become my salvation: he is my God, and I will prepare him an habitation; my father's God, and I will exalt him.

EXODUS 15:2

God is my strength and power: And he maketh my way perfect.

2 SAMUEL 22:23

The Lord is my strength and song, and is become my salvation.

PSALM 118:14

Behold, God is my salvation; I will trust, and not be afraid: for the Lord Jehovah is my strength and my song; he also is become my salvation.

ISAIAH 12:2

For thou hast girded me with strength to battle: them
that rose up against me hast thou subdued under me.
2 SAMUEL 22:40

For thou hast girded me with strength unto the battle:
thou hast subdued under me those that rose up against
me.
PSALM 18:39

Let the words of my mouth, and the meditation of my
heart, be acceptable in thy sight, O Lord, my strength,
and my redeemer.
PSALM 19:14

The Lord will give strength unto his people; the Lord
will bless his people with peace.
PSALM 29:11

Sing aloud unto God our strength: make a joyful noise
unto the God of Jacob.
PSALM 81:1

My flesh and my heart faileth: but God is the strength of
my heart, and my portion for ever.
PSALM 73:26

A wise man is strong; yea, a man of knowledge increaseth strength.
PROVERBS 24:5

Trust ye in the Lord for ever: for in the Lord Jehovah is everlasting strength.
ISAIAH 26:4

He giveth power to the faint; and to them that have no might he increaseth strength.
ISAIAH 40:29

And he said unto me, My grace is sufficient for thee: for my strength is made perfect in weakness. Most gladly therefore will I rather glory in my infirmities, that the power of Christ may rest upon me.
2 CORINTHIANS 12:9

Thy God hath commanded thy strength: strengthen, God, that which thou hast wrought for us.
PSALM 68:28

Finally, my brethren, be strong in the Lord, and in the power of his might.
EPHESIANS 6:10

It is God that girdeth me with strength, and maketh my way perfect.

PSALM 18:32

When You Need Deliverance

Truly my soul waiteth upon God: from him cometh my salvation. He only is my rock and my salvation; he is my defence; I shall not be greatly moved.
PSALM 62:1-2

My soul, wait thou only upon God; for my expectation is from him. He only is my rock and my salvation: he is my defence; I shall not be moved. In God is my salvation and my glory: the rock of my strength, and my refuge, is in God. Trust in him at all times; ye people, pour out your heart before him: God is a refuge for us.
PSALM 62:5-8

God hath spoken once; twice have I heard this; that power belongeth unto God. Also unto thee, O Lord, belongeth mercy: for thou renderest to every man according to his work.
PSALM 62:11-12

The Lord knoweth how to deliver the godly out of temptations, and to reserve the unjust unto the day of judgment to be punished.
2 PETER 2:9

He sent from above, he took me, he drew me out of many waters. He delivered me from my strong enemy, and from them which hated me: for they were too strong for me. They prevented me in the day of my calamity: but the Lord was my stay. He brought me forth also into a large place; he delivered me, because he delighted in me.
PSALM 18:16-19

Thou shalt hide them in the secret of thy presence from the pride of man: thou shalt keep them secretly in a pavilion from the strife of tongues.
PSALM 31:20

I sought the Lord, and he heard me, and delivered me from all my fears.
PSALM 34:4

Many are the afflictions of the righteous: but the Lord delivereth him out of them all.
PSALM 34:19

Then said Jesus to those Jews which believed on him, If ye continue in my word, then are ye my disciples indeed; And ye shall know the truth, and the truth shall make you free.
JOHN 8:31-32

Then he called his twelve disciples together, and gave them power and authority over all devils, and to cure diseases.
LUKE 9:1

And when he had called unto him his twelve disciples, he gave them power against unclean spirits, to cast them out, and to heal all manner of sickness and all manner of disease.
MATTHEW 10:1

When the even was come, they brought unto him many that were possessed with devils: and he cast out the spirits with his word, and healed all that were sick:
That it might be fulfilled which was spoken by Esaias the prophet, saying, Himself took our infirmities, and bare our sicknesses.
MATTHEW 8:16-17

And the Lord shall deliver me from every evil work, and will preserve me unto his heavenly kingdom: to whom be glory for ever and ever. Amen.
2 TIMOTHY 4:18

Behold, I give unto you power to tread on serpents and scorpions, and over all the power of the enemy: and nothing shall by any means hurt you.

LUKE 10:19

When You Have Doubts

As soon as Jesus heard the word that was spoken, he saith unto the ruler of the synagogue, Be not afraid, only believe.
MARK 5:36

Jesus said unto him, If thou canst believe, all things are possible to him that believeth. And straightway the father of the child cried out, and said with tears, Lord, I believe; help thou mine unbelief.
MARK 9:23-24

For verily I say unto you, That whosoever shall say unto this mountain, Be thou removed, and be thou cast into the sea; and shall not doubt in his heart, but shall believe that those things which he saith shall come to pass; he shall have whatsoever he saith.
Therefore I say unto you, What things soever ye desire, when ye pray, believe that ye receive them, and ye shall have them.
MARK 11:23-24

And he said, Lord, I believe. And he worshipped him.
JOHN 9:38

But if I do, though ye believe not me, believe the works:
that ye may know, and believe, that the Father is in me,
and I in him.
JOHN 10:38

Let not your heart be troubled: ye believe in God, believe
also in me.
Believe me that I am in the Father, and the Father in me:
or else believe me for the very works' sake.
JOHN 14:1,11

Jesus answered them, Do ye now believe?
JOHN 16:31

The other disciples therefore said unto him, We have seen
the Lord. But he said unto them, Except I shall see in his
hands the print of the nails, and put my finger into the
print of the nails, and thrust my hand into his side, I will
not believe.
And after eight days again his disciples were within, and
Thomas with them: then came Jesus, the doors being shut,
and stood in the midst, and said, Peace be unto you.
Then saith he to Thomas, Reach hither thy finger, and
behold my hands; and reach hither thy hand, and thrust
it into my side: and be not faithless, but believing.
And Thomas answered and said unto him, My Lord and
my God.
Jesus saith unto him, Thomas, because thou hast seen me,
thou hast believed: blessed are they that have not seen,
and yet have believed.
And many other signs truly did Jesus in the presence of
his disciples, which are not written in this book:
But these are written, that ye might believe that Jesus is
the Christ, the Son of God; and that believing ye might
have life through his name.
JOHN 20:25-31

And when there had been much disputing, Peter rose up, and said unto them, Men and brethren, ye know how that a good while ago God made choice among us, that the Gentiles by my mouth should hear the word of the gospel, and believe.
ACTS 15:7

Wherefore, sirs, be of good cheer: for I believe God, that it shall be even as it was told me.
ACTS 27:25

And he received the sign of circumcision, a seal of the righteousness of the faith which he had yet being uncircumcised: that he might be the father of all them that believe, though they be not circumcised; that righteousness might be imputed unto them also.
ROMANS 4:11

For therefore we both labour and suffer reproach, because we trust in the living God, who is the Saviour of all men, specially of those that believe.
1 TIMOTHY 4:10

But without faith it is impossible to please him: for he that cometh to God must believe that he is, and that he is a rewarder of them that diligently seek him.
HEBREWS 11:6

And this is his commandment, That we should believe on the name of his Son Jesus Christ, and love one another, as he gave us commandment.
1 JOHN 3:23

Now the God of hope fill you with all joy and peace in believing, that ye may abound in hope, through the power of the Holy Ghost.

ROMANS 15:13

Jesus said unto him, If thou canst believe, all things are possible to him that believeth.
MARK 9:23

Beareth all things, believeth all things, hopeth all things, endureth all things.
1 CORINTHIANS 13:7

Then saith he to Thomas, Reach hither thy finger, and behold my hands; and reach hither thy hand, and thrust it into my side: and be not faithless, but believing.
JOHN 20:27

When You Do Not Feel God's Presence

Thou wilt shew me the path of life: in thy presence is fulness of joy; at thy right hand there are pleasures for evermore.
PSALM 16:11

Let your conversation be without covetousness; and be content with such things as ye have: for he hath said, I will never leave thee, nor forsake thee.
HEBREWS 13:5

Greater love hath no man than this, that a man lay down his life for his friends. Ye are my friends, if ye do whatsoever I command you. Henceforth I call you not servants; for the servant knoweth not what his lord doeth: but I have called you friends; for all things that I have heard of my Father I have made known unto you.
JOHN 15:13-15

Have not I commanded thee? Be strong and of a good courage; be not afraid, neither be thou dismayed: for the Lord thy God is with thee whithersoever thou goest.
JOSHUA 1:9

For a great door and effectual is opened unto me, and there are many adversaries.
1 CORINTHIANS 16:9

The Lord is nigh unto all them that call upon him, to all that call upon him in truth.
PSALM 145:18

But without faith it is impossible to please him: for he that cometh to God must believe that he is, and that he is a rewarder of them that diligently seek him.
HEBREWS 11:6

Draw nigh to God, and he will draw nigh to you. Cleanse your hands, ye sinners; and purify your hearts, ye double minded.
JAMES 4:8

Behold, I stand at the door, and knock: if any man hear my voice, and open the door, I will come in to him, and will sup with him, and he with me.
REVELATION 3:20

A man that hath friends must shew himself friendly: and
there is a friend that sticketh closer than a brother.
PROVERBS 18:24

And ye shall seek me, and find me, when ye shall search
for me with all your heart.
JEREMIAH 29:13

The Lord is good unto them that wait for him, to the soul
that seeketh him.
LAMENTATIONS 3:25

All that the Father giveth me shall come to me; and him
that cometh to me I will in no wise cast out.
JOHN 6:37

Repent ye therefore, and be converted, that your sins may
be blotted out, when the times of refreshing shall come
from the presence of the Lord.
ACTS 3:19

And he said, My presence shall go with thee, and I will
give thee rest.
EXODUS 33:14

Teaching them to observe all things whatsoever I have commanded you: and, lo, I am with you always, even unto the end of the world.

MATTHEW 28:20

When You Feel Like a Failure

YOUR PERSONAL NEEDS

I can do all things through Christ which strengtheneth
me.
PHILIPPIANS 4:13

Nay, in all these things we are more than conquerors
through him that loved us.
ROMANS 8:37

For whatsoever is born of God overcometh the world:
and this is the victory that overcometh the world, even
our faith.
1 JOHN 5:4

I will extol thee, O Lord; for thou hast lifted me up, and
hast not made my foes to rejoice over me.
PSALM 30:1

This book of the law shall not depart out of thy mouth;
but thou shalt meditate therein day and night, that thou
mayest observe to do according to all that is written
therein: for then thou shalt make thy way prosperous, and
then thou shalt have good success.
JOSHUA 1:8

But thou, O Lord, art a shield for me; my glory, and the
lifter up of mine head.
PSALM 3:3

The Lord lifteth up the meek: he casteth the wicked down
to the ground.
PSALM 147:6

Ye are of God, little children, and have overcome them:
because greater is he that is in you, than he that is in the
world.
1 JOHN 4:4

Now thanks be unto God, which always causeth us to
triumph in Christ, and maketh manifest the savour of his
knowledge by us in every place.
2 CORINTHIANS 2:14

I am crucified with Christ: nevertheless I live; yet not I,
but Christ liveth in me: and the life which I now live in
the flesh I live by the faith of the Son of God, who loved
me, and gave himself for me.
GALATIANS 2:20

Therefore if any man be in Christ, he is a new creature: old things are passed away; behold, all things are become new.
2 CORINTHIANS 5:17

But I have prayed for thee, that thy faith fail not: and when thou art converted, strengthen thy brethren.
LUKE 22:32

Cast me not off in the time of old age; forsake me not when my strength faileth.
PSALM 71:9

My flesh and my heart faileth: but God is the strength of my heart, and my portion for ever.
PSALM 73:26

And if children, then heirs; heirs of God, and joint-heirs with Christ; if so be that we suffer with him, that we may be also glorified together.
ROMANS 8:17

And if ye be Christ's, then are ye Abraham's seed, and heirs according to the promise.
GALATIANS 3:29

But thanks be to God, which giveth us the victory through our Lord Jesus Christ.

1 CORINTHIANS 15:57

When You Feel Unusual Stress

YOUR PERSONAL NEEDS

Persecuted, but not forsaken; cast down, but not destroyed.
2 CORINTHIANS 4:9

And not only so, but we glory in tribulations also: knowing
that tribulation worketh patience.
ROMANS 5:3

Who shall separate us from the love of Christ? shall
tribulation, or distress, or persecution, or famine, or
nakedness, or peril, or sword?
ROMANS 8:35

Rejoicing in hope; patient in tribulation; continuing instant
in prayer.
ROMANS 12:12

Who comforteth us in all our tribulation, that we may be
able to comfort them which are in any trouble, by the
comfort wherewith we ourselves are comforted of God.
2 CORINTHIANS 1:4

Great is my boldness of speech toward you, great is my glorying of you: I am filled with comfort, I am exceeding joyful in all our tribulation. That the trial of your faith, being much more precious than of gold that perisheth, though it be tried with fire, might be found unto praise and honour and glory at the appearing of Jesus Christ.
1 PETER 1:7

Beloved, think it not strange concerning the fiery trial which is to try you, as though some strange thing happened unto you.
1 PETER 4:12

But and if ye suffer for righteousness' sake, happy are ye: and be not afraid of their terror, neither be troubled.
1 PETER 3:14

These things I have spoken unto you, that in me ye might have peace. In the world ye shall have tribulation: but be of good cheer; I have overcome the world.
JOHN 16:33

For which cause we faint not; but though our outward man perish, yet the inward man is renewed day by day.
2 CORINTHIANS 4:16

In the day of my trouble I will call upon thee: for thou wilt answer me.
PSALM 86:7

The righteous is delivered out of trouble, and the wicked
cometh in his stead.
PROVERBS 11:8

Be careful for nothing; but in every thing by prayer and
supplication with thanksgiving let your requests be made
known unto God.
PHILIPPIANS 4:6

In my distress I called upon the Lord, and cried unto my
God: he heard my voice out of his temple, and my cry
came before him, even into his ears.
PSALM 18:6

In my distress I called upon the Lord, and cried to my
God: and he did hear my voice out of his temple, and my
cry did enter into his ears.
2 SAMUEL 22:7

And the king sware, and said, As the Lord liveth, that
hath redeemed my soul out of all distress.
1 KINGS 1:29

I called upon the Lord in distress: the Lord answered me,
and set me in a large place.
PSALM 118:5

In my distress I cried unto the Lord, and he heard me.

PSALM 120:1

When You Have Bad Memories of the Past

And be not conformed to this world: but be ye transformed by the renewing of your mind, that ye may prove what is that good, and acceptable, and perfect, will of God.
ROMANS 12:2

Therefore if any man be in Christ, he is a new creature: old things are passed away; behold, all things are become new.
2 CORINTHIANS 5:17

Brethren, I count not myself to have apprehended: but this one thing I do, forgetting those things which are behind, and reaching forth unto those things which are before.
PHILIPPIANS 3:13

Behold, I will do a new thing; now it shall spring forth; shall ye not know it? I will even make a way in the wilderness, and rivers in the desert.
ISAIAH 43:19

Behold, the former things are come to pass, and new things do I declare: before they spring forth I tell you of them.
ISAIAH 42:9

For, lo, the winter is past, the rain is over and gone.
SONG OF SOLOMON 2:11

Whom God hath set forth to be a propitiation through faith in his blood, to declare his righteousness for the remission of sins that are past, through the forbearance of God.
ROMANS 3:25

Wherein in time past ye walked according to the course of this world, according to the prince of the power of the air, the spirit that now worketh in the children of disobedience. Among whom also we all had our conversation in times past in the lusts of our flesh, fulfilling the desires of the flesh and of the mind; and were by nature the children of wrath, even as others.
EPHESIANS 2:2-3

And be renewed in the spirit of your mind.
EPHESIANS 4:23

That he might sanctify and cleanse it with the washing of water by the word.
EPHESIANS 5:26

When Your Want to Be Close to God

The Lord is good unto them that wait for him, to the soul
that seeketh him.
LAMENTATIONS 3:25

Draw nigh to God, and he will draw nigh to you. Cleanse
your hands, ye sinners; and purify your hearts, ye double
minded.
JAMES 4:8

But if from thence thou shalt seek the Lord thy God, thou
shalt find him, if thou seek him with all thy heart and
with all thy soul.
DEUTERONOMY 4:29

And he sought God in the days of Zechariah, who had
understanding in the visions of God: and as long as he
sought the Lord, God made him to prosper.
2 CHRONICLES 26:5

One thing have I desired of the Lord, that will I seek after; that I may dwell in the house of the Lord all the days of my life, to behold the beauty of the Lord, and to inquire in his temple.
For in the time of trouble he shall hide me in his pavilion: in the secret of his tabernacle shall he hide me; he shall set me up upon a rock.
And now shall mine head be lifted up above mine enemies round about me: therefore will I offer in his tabernacle sacrifices of joy; I will sing, yea, I will sing praises unto the Lord.
Hear, O Lord, when I cry with my voice: have mercy also upon me, and answer me.
When thou saidst, Seek ye my face; my heart said unto thee, Thy face, Lord, will I seek.

PSALM 27:4-8

As the hart panteth after the water brooks, so panteth my soul after thee, O God. My soul thirsteth for God, for the living God: when shall I come and appear before God?

PSALM 42:1-2

O God, thou art my God; early will I seek thee: my soul thirsteth for thee, my flesh longeth for thee in a dry and thirsty land, where no water is; To see thy power and thy glory, so as I have seen thee in the sanctuary.

PSALM 63:1-2

The Lord is nigh unto all them that call upon him, to all
that call upon him in truth.
PSALM 145:18

For they got not the land in possession by their own
sword, neither did their own arm save them: but thy right
hand, and thine arm, and the light of thy countenance,
because thou hadst a favour unto them.
PSALM 44:3

Blessed are they which do hunger and thirst after righteousness: for they shall be filled.
MATTHEW 5:6

That they should seek the Lord, if haply they might feel
after him, and find him, though he be not far from every
one of us.
ACTS 17:27

And the Spirit and the bride say, Come. And let him that
heareth say, Come. And let him that is athirst come. And
whosoever will, let him take the water of life freely.
REVELATION 22:17

And ye shall seek me, and find me, when ye shall search for me with all your heart.

JEREMIAH 29:13

When You Do Not Feel Like God Hears You

YOUR PERSONAL NEEDS

And I have also heard the groaning of the children of Israel, whom the Egyptians keep in bondage; and I have remembered my covenant.
EXODUS 6:5

If my people, which are called by my name, shall humble themselves, and pray, and seek my face, and turn from their wicked ways; then will I hear from heaven, and will forgive their sin, and will heal their land.
2 CHRONICLES 7:14

Thou shalt make thy prayer unto him, and he shall hear thee, and thou shalt pay thy vows.
JOB 22:27

And they that know thy name will put their trust in thee: for thou, Lord, hast not forsaken them that seek thee.
PSALM 9:10

Lord, thou hast heard the desire of the humble: thou wilt
prepare their heart, thou wilt cause thine ear to hear.
PSALM 10:17

The eyes of the Lord are upon the righteous, and his ears
are open unto their cry.
The righteous cry, and the Lord heareth, and delivereth
them out of all their troubles.
PSALM 34:15,17

Evening, and morning, and at noon, will I pray, and cry
aloud: and he shall hear my voice.
PSALM 55:17

O thou that hearest prayer, unto thee shall all flesh come.
PSALM 65:2

Again I say unto you, That if two of you shall agree on
earth as touching any thing that they shall ask, it shall
be done for them of my Father which is in heaven.
For where two or three are gathered together in my name,
there am I in the midst of them.
MATTHEW 18:19-20

For the Lord heareth the poor, and despiseth not his
prisoners.
PSALM 69:33

He will regard the prayer of the destitute, and not despise
their prayer.
PSALM 102:17

The Lord is nigh unto all them that call upon him, to all
that call upon him in truth. He will fulfill the desire of
them that fear him: he also will hear their cry, and will
save them.
PSALM 145:18-19

And it shall come to pass, that before they call, I will
answer; and while they are yet speaking, I will hear.
ISAIAH 65:24

Call unto me, and I will answer thee, and shew thee great
and mighty things, which thou knowest not.
JEREMIAH 33:3

And I will bring the third part through the fire, and will
refine them as silver is refined, and will try them as gold
is tried: they shall call on my name, and I will hear them:
I will say, It is my people: and they shall say, The Lord is
my God.
ZECHARIAH 13:9

But thou, when thou prayest, enter into thy closet, and
when thou hast shut thy door, pray to thy Father which
is in secret; and thy Father which seeth in secret shall
reward thee openly.
Be not ye therefore like unto them: for your Father knoweth
what things ye have need of, before ye ask him.
MATTHEW 6:6,8

Give ear, O Lord, unto my prayer; and attend to the voice of my supplications.

PSALM 86:6

When People Think You Are Weird

YOUR PERSONAL NEEDS

But he is a Jew, which is one inwardly; and circumcision is that of the heart, in the spirit, and not in the letter; whose praise is not of men, but of God.
ROMANS 2:29

Therefore judge nothing before the time, until the Lord come, who both will bring to light the hidden things of darkness, and will make manifest the counsels of the hearts: and then shall every man have praise of God.
1 CORINTHIANS 4:5

For they loved the praise of men more than the praise of God.
JOHN 12:43

For the time past of our life may suffice us to have wrought the will of the Gentiles, when we walked in lasciviousness, lusts, excess of wine, re veilings, banquetings, and abominable idolatries: Wherein they think it strange that ye run not with them to the same excess of riot, speaking evil of you.
1 PETER 4:3-4

If ye were of the world, the world would love his own: but because ye are not of the world, but I have chosen you out of the world, therefore the world hateth you.
JOHN 15:19

Then Peter and the other apostles answered and said, We ought to obey God rather than men.

Great Mothers of the Bible

EVE | MARY | SARAH | HANNAH
ELIZABETH

Eve, First Mother

And Adam called his wife's name Eve; because she was
the mother of all living.
GENESIS 3:20

Mary, Mother of Jesus

And Mary said, My soul doth magnify the Lord,
And my spirit hath rejoiced in God my Saviour.
For he hath regarded the low estate of his handmaiden:
for, behold, from henceforth all generations shall call me
blessed.
For he that is mighty hath done to me great things; and
holy is his name.
And his mercy is on them that fear him from generation
to generation.
He hath shewed strength with his arm; he hath scattered
the proud in the imagination of their hearts.
He hath put down the mighty from their seats, and exalted
them of low degree.
He hath filled the hungry with good things; and the rich
he hath sent empty away.
He hath holpen his servant Israel, in remembrance of his
mercy;
As he spake to our fathers, to Abraham, and to his seed
for ever.
LUKE 1:46-55

Sarah, Mother of Isaac

For Sarah conceived, and bare Abraham a son in his old
age, at the set time of which God had spoken to him.
And Abraham called the name of his son that was born
unto him, whom Sarah bare to him, Isaac.
GENESIS 21:2-3

Hannah, Mother of Samuel

And she said, Oh my lord, as thy soul liveth, my lord, I
am the woman that stood by thee here, praying unto the
Lord. For this child I prayed; and the Lord hath given me
my petition which I asked of him: Therefore also I have
lent him to the Lord; as long as he liveth he shall be lent
to the Lord. And he worshipped the Lord there.
1 SAMUEL 1:26-28

Elizabeth, Mother of John the Baptist

And she spake out with a loud voice, and said, Blessed art
thou among women, and blessed is the fruit of thy womb.
LUKE 1:42